Table of Contents

PREFACE

Why should you invest the time to read this book?

The compact book you are holding is intended as a practical guide to managers and supervisors in the first two to three years of their tenure. Professionals who aspire to management will also find it useful. It outlines the main missteps that most newly-appointed managers make – and offers specific, every day practices to avoid or overcome those missteps.

It is compact, because you don't have a lot of time for reading – given that you are probably struggling to strike a balance between continuing your technical contributions and mastering the demands of management. It is compact, because unlike most management books sold today, it is not artificially lengthened by case studies and interview data of dubious relevance. Instead, you will be provided with personal, real-life examples and illustrations to illuminate and make relevant the practice or principle being discussed.

It is practical, because as a former manager who struggled with my own transition into management, I know that you need actionable advice, not more theories. Some of the material is derived from my own experience as a manager. Another source is the experience of the hundreds of participants in my "Transitioning from Individual Contributor to Manager" workshop. Over the past ten years they have regularly reminded me that the transition is not an easy one-- and that most of the books they've consulted haven't helped much. In session after session their candid remarks about their transitions also have alerted me to the fact that the initiation into management is getting more, not less, challenging.

So, why read this book?

Read it if:

- You are struggling with the dual demands of doing vs. managing.

- You are not yet clear about the strengths and areas for development of your management style.

- You want to create a productive climate within your group, but find it challenging.

- You want to be a better coach.

- You aspire to excellence and want to develop your leadership capabilities.

For your convenience I have concluded each chapter with "Notes" that capture the main points of the section. Also included are "Application Exercises" that facilitate transference to your work environment. You will derive greater benefit from the book if you take the time to reflect and act on the Exercises. So resist the temptation to move too quickly through the chapters. The material will yield real on-the-job results for you only if you carefully consider the practices and reflect on how you can begin applying them.

CHAPTER 1

FAILING TO LET GO

Letting go of your old job is the necessary first step to transitioning into management, but it is a step many fail to make well. In fact, some never fully let go of their old role and so fail to really commit to their new responsibilities. This transition, moving from the mentality and habits of an individual contributor to that of a manager, is challenging for several of the following reasons:

HABITS

If you are like most people, you were promoted within your group, or at least your division or business unit. You learned the ropes, got things done, and so were elevated to manager. Yet you remained in the same or similar environment, an environment where your habits are well-formed and your routines set. But now you have new responsibilities. In this situation, most of us unconsciously try to do the new job while holding on to the old ways of behaving and old habits of mind. Many newly appointed managers even resent the new time-consuming tasks that running a group entails. Participants in my "Transitioning from Individual Contributor to Manager" seminar frequently voice complaints such as: "All I seem to wind up doing is attend meetings, listen to people and deal with personnel issues."

In short, they are complaining that their responsibilities are infringing on their old duties, the duties that are familiar and comfortable. They are trying to hold on to the old and familiar while trying to tackle the new. Not surprisingly, they report that they end up working long hours, worrying a lot, and neglecting their management tasks.

PERFORMANCE PRESSURE

Most people get promoted because they are technically proficient. That's probably why you got the job of manager. And even though they know you have new responsibilities, your internal customers, and others who benefited from your contributions, will show in numerous ways that they want your contributions to continue. Without saying as much, they are urging you to "keep it up," in other words, continue to function as an individual contributor. Your old habits, as well as the messages from others, incline you to hold on to your old ways of working and to your old responsibilities.

Even your boss can contribute to your dilemma. He/she will often admonish you to "let go" of the technical while at the same time continuing to expect no interruptions in productivity from your group. You are expected to "get others up to speed" quickly, a feat that often takes more time than the environment allows. So you, the technical whiz, are tempted to "do it yourself."

TRAINING

You were trained in sales or to be an engineer, accountant or scientist, -- not a manager. You chose your career path because the issues of your field interest you and because you like to create solutions and solve problems. You like to get things done and make things work; technical challenges motivate you. Your training and your initial on-the-job experiences provided you with skills and know-how and, even more, with an identity. Gradually, you came to view yourself in terms of your role, your activities and achievements. Your sense of who you are became related to what you do. (It's for this reason that many find retirement so difficult: their work defined who they are, now the work is gone, so who are they?) Transitioning into the new role of manager involves seeing yourself differently, creating a new identity—a new identity few of us were prepared or trained for.

To accomplish such a transition you should expect to apply the same learning processes that you employed in becoming an excellent technical contributor: researching, watching, experimenting and seeking feedback. Your technical skills are based on a foundation of basics and principles that you obtained from courses, books and manuals. The skills of management also require research of a sort. Seek out and reflect on management-related articles (for writings on both theory and practice, The Harvard Business Review is consistently helpful). Many best selling business books display more flash and faddishness than insight, but each year authors offer several that are thought provoking and useful.

Observing the practices of other managers is even more productive. Cultivate the habit of ascertaining the most noteworthy abilities of successful managers in your organization. Note how each of them uses their skills and then adopt after adapting. By this I mean experimenting with the practice of management in ways that are compatible with your style. You don't have to do it just like he/she does it (and probably shouldn't for reasons we will explore in the next chapter). By closely observing the practices of others and then tailoring them to fit your operating style you can pick up valuable approaches in making requests, asking questions, listening, running meetings, negotiating, dealing with conflict and all the other numerous activities of management. A fuller exploration of this kind of learning will be provided in Chapter Seven. Seeking feedback is also critical in the learning process. Enlist partners, co-workers you like and trust, in the effort. Ask them to candidly evaluate your meetings, presentations and negotiations. If you show receptivity to their observations and avoid pushing back or defending your behavior, you will obtain valuable data. Don't fear critical feedback, learn to live with it and learn from it.

RECOGNITION

As an individual contributor, there was an easily discernible link between your efforts (input) and the results (output). You saw the results and others did as well. Your goals for the most part were clear and defined and you got recognition from peers and bosses. The recognition reinforced your belief that beyond just making a living, you were making a difference. You began to see yourself as useful, even important, because you and others saw what you produced. Letting go of the work, the source of your recognition and motivation, is not just a question of breaking old habits or learning time management, it is a question of discovering new sources of motivation. Formerly, you derived satisfaction and motivation from producing; now, you must learn to derive satisfaction and motivation from somewhere else – from helping others produce and succeed. This internal reordering and redefining is not easy – in fact, many managers never really make it. They perform the tasks of management, but are motivated by the rewards associated with doing, the rewards of the individual contributor. Because they have not truly shifted to a managerial mentality, they dabble in the technical to get satisfaction. In the process, they can fall prey to micro-management and steal the thunder of the people they manage.

The essence of this transition is letting go of the old pay-off's and embracing a new motivation system for yourself. Truly becoming a manager means seeing yourself as a facilitator of the productivity and success of others, and deriving your motivation and sense of value from this new role.

WHAT TO DO:

Find new sources of motivation

To overcome the obstacles to a successful transition into management, obstacles created by habits, the expectations of other people, and your very natural attachment to your old activities, you will have to develop new sources of inspiration and motivation. Formerly, accomplishing specific tasks motivated you, now you must find ways to derive motivation from assisting others. This is not easy. The world of sport demonstrates just how difficult this shift can be.

Larry Bird was an all-star basketball player in college and for the Boston Celtics in the NBA. After an award-studded playing career, he became the coach of the Indiana Pacers in the NBA. But when he completed three successful seasons as a coach, Bird abruptly resigned. At the time, he said he quit because "after a few years, they don't listen to you anymore." Later, with the benefit of a few years of reflection, he wrote an autobiography in which he revealed the real reason for his decision. There he reported that he couldn't stand the discomfort of being on the bench in a suit and tie while the game was being decided. He wanted to play, he wanted the ball, and he wanted to score points. Larry Bird, the coach, remained in his heart of hearts, an individual contributor. He longed for the days when his actions directly decided outcomes, like the playoff game he had played in as a Boston Celtic. With little time left, his coach, K.C. Jones, had called a time out and proceeded to draw up an elaborate play for winning the game. Bird interrupted his coach and when Jones looked at him, Bird simply said: "Just get me the damn ball." After a moment, Jones nodded, so did the rest of the team. Then Bird went out, made the shot – and won the game.

Even if you are not a sports fan, you can appreciate the relevance of Bird's experience. He couldn't let go of doing. Or to put it another way, as a coach he never really learned to appreciate the contribution he was making as a coach. What he failed to do is what you have to master: be able to watch the team members succeed and know that you, their manager, helped make it possible. Your planning, direction setting, coaching and example contributed to the team's effectiveness – even if you did not score a point. You are present in the game through your influence, not through your play. You help decide the outcomes in an indirect, yet real way. You have to learn to be motivated by the team's performance, and have to develop the ability to look at the "scoreboard" and know that, without making points, you helped win the game.

Have a candid conversation about your transition with your boss.

Your boss is worried about you. He/she will probably not voice those concerns, but they are there. Your boss knows that the transition is challenging and wonders how you will handle it, but will probably avoid saying anything that might undermine your confidence. So most bosses of newly appointed managers just watch and wait. You should take the initiative. Get an appointment with him/her and explore the following topics:

- His/her main expectations – what does he/she want from you in this new position?

- What should your Doer/Manager ratio be?

- What skills does he/she think you should concentrate on?

- What kinds of issues should you bring to him/her; where do you have complete freedom to act?

Finally, show a willingness to be coached. Assure him/her that you will be open to observations and suggestions. This assurance will go a long way toward forming a real partnership between you and your manager. This partnership is vital to your success because without the support of a boss, few new managers will be effective.

Honestly assess your management strengths and target areas for development

Your track record as a doer has given you a well-deserved sense of satisfaction with your skills. You know what you can do well – as a doer. Fine. That chapter is now over. From now on even when you make technical contributions you will notice that others will seldom give you acknowledgement or praise – doer abilities are now a given. What others will take note of and judge are your management skills. To some extent, bosses and peers, but especially subordinates, will pay attention to these activities:

- The quality of your decisions

- Your ability to set direction and speak with clarity

- Your listening

- Your delegation

- The effectiveness of your meetings

- Your coaching

- Your ability to deal with reversals and critical feedback

Others will be observing and evaluating your performance in these matters and so should you. You need to get very clear about your management strengths and experiment with ways to leverage them and also identify the areas for improvement.

We will provide some guidelines for this process of self-evaluation later in the chapter. For now it is critical that you realize that the yardstick has changed. You will have to focus on new skills and begin to measure yourself differently.

Analyze your use of time

Every new manager has to master the balancing act: juggling technical contributions with management activities. Staying involved in the work of your group is necessary; staying too involved will incline you to neglect your new management tasks. Finding your balance is not easy, it demands close analysis.

One indication of how well you have let go of your old job and focused on your new responsibilities is the amount of time you spend on doing versus managing. Although there is no ratio that applies equally to all situations, there is an appropriate mix for you.

Reflect on the last week. Look through your calendar. Determine how many hours you spent in managing as opposed to doing.

MANAGING ACTIVITIES

_____ Planning

_____ Coaching

_____ Participating in meetings

_____ Coordinating with other groups

_____ Discussions with boss

_____ One-on-one's with group members

_____ Total

DOER ACTIVITIES

_____ Developing products

_____ Fire fighting

_____ Dealing with customers (external and internal)

_____ Debugging, technical problem-solving

_____ Total

Now ask yourself if this ratio is right for your situation. Consider the following:

- Is the group becoming more/less productive?

- How satisfied are your main customers?

- How does your boss view the group?

- Do the group members have a good sense of direction? Are priorities clear?

- Are problems quickly identified and addressed?

- Are group members developing critical skills?

- How good is morale?

After considering these questions ask yourself if your allocation of time, energy and attention is right for your situation. If your answers to the above questions leave you unsatisfied, you probably are not managing enough.

Evaluate your current "pay-off's"

The "pay-off's" of being a manager are very different from those coming to an individual contributor. Everyone works for pay-off's beyond salary and benefits. In short, we all want to feel that what we are doing is making a difference. If you are not deriving satisfaction from your management efforts, you will find pay-off's elsewhere – usually in doer or individual contributor activities.

Look over the following lists and honestly assess where your "juice" comes from, which pay-off's really motivate and inspire you.

TYPICAL ADVANTAGES/PAYOFFS OF INDIVIDUAL CONTRIBUTOR

- Sense of accomplishment: getting things done

- Concrete results

- Viewed as expert

- Can keep technical skills honed

- Clear goals

- Positive feedback

- Limited responsibility

- Focus on one's own projects

- Freedom to complain, blame "them" (management)

TYPICAL ADVANTAGES/PAYOFFS OF MANAGER

- Set direction

- Access to information

- View of "Big picture"

- Control of resources

- Ability to make decisions

- Developing others

- Learn "people skills"

- Broad responsibilities

- Ability to leverage: get more done through other people

Even a cursory consideration of these lists reveals an important truth: the pay-off's of management while significant and longer term, are more abstract and difficult to see – and appreciate. In other words, the impact of management can seem obscure, indirect, even hidden. On the other hand, when an engineer successfully debugs a system, a salesperson wins a new account or a scientist publishes his hard-won findings – such individual contributor achievements are easy to see and appreciate. And they are rewarded. These concrete pay-off's can be seductive and many new managers succumb – unless they learn to derive satisfaction and motivation from the broader and longer term, albeit harder to see, pay-off's.

Here's the tough question: where does your motivation currently come from, list one or list two. Until you begin to derive more satisfaction from empowering others, guiding others and coaching them to new levels of productivity, you will be tempted to get your motivation from "doer" activities and not really make the transition to a managerial mind set.

Evaluate your skill level

Gauge your current level of proficiency in each of the following areas by rating your current level on a 1-7 scale. 7 = almost always, 1 = hardly ever.

Self-awareness and Flexibility

I can see myself as others do

I readily adjust to differences

I know my values and act on them

I can list my strengths at work

I am aware of my deficiencies

Time and Energy Management

I am able to stay focused on key priorities

I show endurance in the face of obstacles

I have minimized the impact of time wasters in my work life

I generally control my emotions

I can project commitment and enthusiasm

Direction and Focus

I have established a basic strategy and a few key goals for myself and my group

I know how to keep my group aligned

I delegate effectively

I can show my group the "big picture"

I make my expectations known

Communication

I can create a network of support with peers

I have reached basic alignment with my boss

I show others that I'm listening

I can put my opinions and assumptions aside to consider another point of view

I can make assertive, non-aggressive requests

Group Management

I make sure each meeting has an agenda

I encourage participation

I keep meetings on track

I keep the group informed about divisional and company issues

I identify and deal with problems in the group

This list of twenty-five management functions is not all-inclusive, but can serve as the basis of a process of self-appraisal. To begin, choose one area that is a strength and come up with specific practices that will help leverage that asset. An aggregate rating of over 30 in an area would usually be a strength. Also, select one of the areas that could be improved and set a few development goals for yourself.

Do not hesitate to enlist your boss in your development. After a period of 3-6 months on the job, take the initiative and get the perceptions and suggestions of your boss. Such an initiative will demonstrate your openness to coaching and may get you invaluable suggestions. I remember approaching my boss early in my first management job. In response, he mentioned administrative practices that I gave scant attention to, but that he, a highly organized and structured person saw as critical. His feedback encouraged me to pay more attention to orderliness and follow-up. This attention to detail and process not only increased my efficiency, but helped equip me to gain promotions in the future.

Seeking feedback from your boss has another advantage. If he/she, has an Operating Style different from yours, he/she will see things you may miss. Each of us has blind spots, aspects of our work style that we may not be aware of. Determining what those blind spots are and deciding on steps to counter them early in your career will increase your confidence and effectiveness as a manager.

Notes

Chapter One

Habits, training and requests from internal customers can incline you to "hold on" to your old job.

Learning how to manage effectively requires effort:

Watch other managers to pick up techniques

Seek feedback, don't pretend to know everything

Focus on the pay-off's of managing as opposed to those of individual contributor activities in order to realign your motivation:

- Building a team
- Coaching others
- Setting direction

Discuss your transition with your boss:

- Clarify his/her expectations
- Discuss the ratio of doing vs. managing
- Clarify the extent of your freedom to act
- Determine which new skills you need to develop
- Honestly gauge your strengths in specific management skills and determine:
- How to leverage strengths
- Compensate for weaknesses

Application Assignment:

- ✓ Fill out the chapter's questionnaires

- ✓ Get feedback from your boss on current strengths and weaknesses

CHAPTER 2

DOING IT LIKE YOUR PREDECESSOR

Each of us has to discover our own way of managing. The trouble is that almost all of us have to clarify and solidify our style of management "on the fly," while doing the job of manager. Rarely do organizations really prepare new managers – most of us are left with trial and error as our method for establishing an approach. On our own we have to figure out how we will run meetings, set goals, deal with bosses, handle performance problems, manage peer relationships, spend time, set priorities – the list is endless and the choices are numerous. Many times, by default, we follow, at least in part, the path established by the person who preceded us. This is especially true if we were promoted from within the group and had watched him or her in action.

Following, consciously or unconsciously, the methods of a predecessor can have an advantage: it's easy. For example, if the way he/she established goals and set direction was successful, why not imitate? But there's a catch, a disadvantage. If his/her operating style, a combination of preferences, skills and strengths, is very different from yours, you will not be successful in following their lead. The challenge is this: to selectively incorporate those elements of their approach that works for you because they fit your style, and alter those that don't.

To navigate through this selection process you have to become actively aware of your preferences, strengths and weaknesses.

Know yourself: Clarifying your Operating Style

As we said, in order to make informed choices about how you will operate as a manager, you have to get clear about your operating style.

What is an Operating Style?

Each of us is unique. Genetic make up, parental influences, formative experiences and preferences make each of us unique. But even though we are unique, we commonly meet people who seem in varying degrees to be like us. Especially at work, certain individuals, talk, think and make decisions in ways that we find easy to adjust to. More often than not, those we find easy to adjust to are like us. In some important ways we share tendencies with them that can be grouped into categories called Operating Styles.

Your Operating Style is your "hard wiring". Time, experience and concerted effort can alter your style, but your tendencies, preferences, strengths, and weaknesses will always be there.

Why is knowing your Operating Style important?

If you adopt practices and approaches from others, especially your predecessor, that are incompatible with your "hard wiring," the practices won't work. For example, some people are highly effective at painting "the big picture." They use colorful language, make creative use of metaphors and relate interesting stories to clarify and persuade. They can operate successfully in this manner because they do it in a skillful manner and they are skilled at it because it's a component of their style. The same statements or actions by others would not work – flair is not part of their style. Such behavior or manner of speaking can be learned, but it will never be easy or natural for someone with a different style. To repeat, knowing your style, your natural tendencies, strengths and preferences is the critical first step in figuring out how you can best operate as a manager – otherwise you could blindly and ineffectively mimic the behavior of others – and fail. Finally, knowing your style helps you identify and more fully leverage your natural strengths, the keys to your success as a manager.

What is your Style?

A quick and effective way to determine your Operating Style is to consider the following questions. After reading them, determine which of the four groupings best describes you at work.

- Are you best at giving specific direction?

- Are you known for being practical?

- Do you like to solve problems?

    - Are you best at analyzing data?

    - Are you known for being objective and analytical?

    - Do you like to set up processes?

- Are you best at forging ties with people?

- Are you known for being sympathetic and a good listener?

- Do you like harmony and cooperation?

    - Are you best at creating new approaches?

    - Are you known for your creativity and "big picture" thinking?

    - Do you like to design models, and propose breakthrough ideas?

If the questions in group one best describe you – you are a Director; if the second sounds like you, you are an Administrator; third, an Integrator; fourth, a Catalyst. Members of each of these style groups can be effective managers, if they fully exploit their style's strengths and manage its weaknesses.

Strengths and Weakness of each Style

DIRECTOR

If you are a Director, you are an effective problem-solver. Someone else telling you how to do something is viewed by you as a challenge to your resourcefulness. You take on assignments with vigor and confidence. In fact, your confidence is your biggest asset. You are a practical tactician who can tolerate theory but would rather focus on the issue at hand by attacking it based on your own experience. You quickly define the problem and begin taking steps to solve it - alone or with a select band of go-getters like yourself. You can slow down to plan, but prefer to plan as you go along. You sometimes surprise others by abruptly changing directions, but you are not troubled by inconsistency; you view such shifts as appropriate responses to a changing situation. Extensive details and background information usually bore you; you prefer action. Finally, your confidence inclines you to resist attempts by others, including your boss, to tell you how to proceed. Someone else telling you how is viewed by you as a challenge to your resourcefulness. You can figure out the best way to go.

ADMINISTRATOR

If Directors excel at tactics and tasks, Administrators are masters of logistics and process. As an Administrator, you need, in fact, require data and a plan before you take action. Your first concern is whether this new problem or opportunity is the right one to focus on, so you ask for data. Your next priority is mapping out how to proceed. You want results but want to make sure that you are "doing it right," that you are using the appropriate people and resources. Because you are process-oriented, you naturally want to know how the steps of the plan will unfold – before starting. From your environment, you require stability, from your boss, clarity, from your co-workers, dependability. You are open to change, although not as open as a Director, but only if the rationale is apparent. That's because you place a great deal of value on the processes already in place. They help ensure efficiency, fairness and continuity – you believe your organization needs processes to function smoothly and you defend them vigorously. You pride yourself on being sensible, objective and dedicated.

INTEGRATOR

Integrators believe that beyond actions or processes, it is people and their level of buy-in and commitment that make an organization work. Directors depend on energy, Administrators on data and Integrators on relationships. If you are an Integrator you value trust, loyalty and openness. If people communicated more effectively, you believe, the organization would thrive. You are viewed as empathetic and approachable because you listen well. People sense that you connect with them and that you care. You worry about how people perceive you because you feel that trust and respect, in short, the quality of your relationships, ultimately determines your effectiveness when working with others. Like the Director, and, unlike the Administrator, you are quite flexible regarding methods, but like to be included in decisions and prefer to be consulted often. Decisions imposed on you are experienced by you as a lack of respect for your professionalism. You frequently are able to find a middle ground between contending factions and can facilitate harmony with your tolerance. You create energy in a group through your involvement and enthusiasm. When needing help you easily win the cooperation of people in other parts of the organization; you are a natural diplomat.

CATALYSTS

In corporate environments, in fact, in most organizations, catalysts are in a distinct minority. Unlike the other Styles that operate in varying degrees "where the rubber meets the road", Catalysts work "where the rubber meets the blue sky". If you are a Catalyst, you are attracted to breakthrough ideas and big picture thinking. You easily see where developments are leading and you excel at creating strategies. In fact, creating is your forte. You like to explore "what ifs" and reach into the future. You are often a model-builder. It is your job to create order out of seeming disorder. You like to sell ideas and inspire people, implementation and detailed follow-up, on the other hand, are much less appealing. You get bored easily and are usually on the lookout for something new. You energize others with possibilities. You are never satisfied with the present, because, for you, it could always be better. You like to be consulted by other groups, in fact, are motivated when other parts of the organization show interest in your ideas and invite your input. Your ideas may not be accepted in totality, but you still feel you have made a contribution to the organization if you have created energy for improvement and change in others – that's why you are called a catalyst.

From the brief overview of the Operating Styles it should be clear that we are all not wired the same. Later we will explore how, as a manager, you can develop the techniques for adjusting to all the styles. For now it is critical that you see that merely "following" in your predecessor's footsteps will not often work. If his/her style is different from yours, you will have to adapt before you adopt.

WHAT TO DO

Remain conscious of your natural strengths. As a manager your impact will be greatest when you fully exploit your strengths.

DIRECTORS excel when they:

- Focus on action.

- Lead by example: their energy and commitment are contagious.

- Encourage flexibility in pursuit of objectives in their reports.

ADMINISTRATORS excel when they:

- Base decisions on good data.

- Lead by example: their constancy and dedication encourages hard work from others.

- Remain objective and even-handed.

INTEGRATORS excel when they:

- Create and maintain networks throughout the organization.

- Lead by example: show respect through courtesy and good listening.

- Involve others and share information.

CATALYSTS excel when they:

- Continue to ask: "what if" questions.

- Lead by example: their energy and restlessness keeps others alert.

- Bring up opportunities not seen by others.

While it is true that leveraging your style's strengths is key to your managerial success, it is also important to attend to your natural weaknesses. The following lists make clear that everyone, no matter what their style, has tendencies and preferences that must be managed, even controlled. In fact the very qualities that win promotions for us can work against us as managers.

MINIMIZE YOUR WEAKNESSES

DIRECTORS need to:

- Consider all angles before deciding.

- Collect more data than they may think is necessary.

- Keep others informed.

- Be patient with people who are not as quick they are.

- Listen, listen, listen.

ADMINISTRATORS need to:

- Tolerate, even encourage differences.

- Open their thinking to include new possibilities.

- Avoid too much structure and micro-management.

- Take risks.

- See the upside in change and new initiatives.

INTEGRATORS need to:

- Deal with tough issues.

- Establish and stay focused on top priorities.

- Be more direct in their speech.

- Avoid taking criticism too personally.

- Manage their time, provide structure to their meetings.

CATALYSTS need to:

- Adhere to deadlines and fulfill promises.

- Provide data and specifics when presenting ideas.

- Follow-up.

- Avoid jumping from one "campaign" to another.

- Think through the implications of implementing their ideas.

Before going to the next section, give some serious reflection to your style. Manifestations of your style are, or shortly will be, apparent to your group members and peers. Others are watching you. They may appreciate your strengths, but they will certainly critique your shortcomings – such scrutiny is part of being a manager. It's critical that you become aware of your pluses and minuses. If you don't, you will be operating at a distinct disadvantage; others will see you more clearly than you will. Reflect on how your strengths come through in one-on-one's and meetings; how your speech is influenced by your style; how you handle conflict and differences; how your style colors your view of others. After critical meetings, and conversations with your boss or important peers ask yourself what went well or poorly. Determine how you could manage your style better the next time you face similar situations. Notice which approaches work best with members of your team, which ones seem to fall flat. Experiment using your knowledge of your style tendencies as a base.

Notes

Chapter Two

Learn from your predecessor, but don't automatically adopt his/her approach.

Determine your Operating Style

- *Main tendencies*
- *Strengths/weaknesses*
- *Decision-making approach*
- *Communication strengths*

Adapt before you adopt

Always, always, remain conscious of your style tendencies

- *Exploit strengths, but don't overuse*
- *Attend to weaknesses*

APPLICATION EXERCISE:

✓ Reflect on the style of your predecessor: list his/her strengths? How did he/she communicate? How did he/she spend time and set priorities? Which of the four styles best describes him/her?

✓ List the similarities and differences between you.

✓ Decide which of his/her key practices fit your style and which should be avoided.

CHAPTER 3

EXPECTING THEM TO DO IT YOUR WAY

John Wooden, legendary coach at UCLA and winner of many national basketball championships, knows a great deal about success and managing people. Once, when asked for insights learned as a coach that could apply to management, Wooden said: "Well, over thirty years of coaching taught me one thing – you can't coach everyone the same way." Now, Wooden did not allow his people to "do their own thing." On the contrary, he instituted rules and enforced them. He once informed Bill Walton – yes, **the** Bill Walton, who is in the Basketball Hall of Fame – that he would have to leave the team if he failed to shave off a beard. Another former UCLA player once told me that during his four years on the team the first half of every practice was exactly the same – a series of basic drills. When I asked why Wooden would insist on such mind-numbing repetition, the former player said: "we were all hot shots, stars; he wanted to show us that he was in charge." Yet Wooden was attentive and responsive to differences among his team members. He knew, or rather, he learned, that different people listen differently, react differently, and he attempted to find the most appropriate and effective way to deal with each individual. To those who needed it, he was direct and forceful; with others he was subtle. He gradually came to see that if he wanted to get through to everyone, he would have to adjust his approach to fit each individual. Getting through, obtaining a hearing is not just a matter of being clear, although that is critical; getting through entails saying it in a way the other will really hear. As you tackle the management of people you will have to develop the ability to depart from your favored style-based approach and use one that gets through to **this** person, in **this** situation. Here's how you can avoid "making them do it your way" and instead bring out the best in others.

Observe tendencies in others and, adjust your approach

Effective management requires attending to all the people you depend on: direct reports, peers and bosses. Cultivate the habit of observing how people act and note which approaches work with each individual. You'll notice, for example, that some prefer clear, short and direct conversations, and are most engaged by practical considerations and specific problems. These people probably are Directors and will be amenable to brief action – oriented approaches. Don't bore them with details. Provide background only if they need the information to understand the issue. Stick to who will do what by when. In dealing with Directors who report to you, concentrate on being very clear about what you want and ask for it directly. Whenever possible, show confidence in their ability and, if they have the requisite skills and background, allow them freedom to figure out for themselves how they will proceed. They don't like to be told how to do something and may even regard detailed direction as a reflection of a lack of confidence by the advice giver. When they perform effectively give them concise, unadorned reinforcement – stick to the facts because they are suspicious of excessive praise and may even look upon it as manipulation. You may not like to be managed like this, but subordinates who are Directors will usually respond favorably.

Administrators will require much more detail, structure and background. They will need more time to reach decisions and will ask a lot of questions about how and why. In many ways they operate and listen and make decisions very differently from Directors. They require plans, data and a process before they start. You will have to spend more time up front with an Administrator, but thoroughness on your part will pay off. Well-prepared Administrators will always come through. They take their commitments and deadlines very seriously and if "won over," they will stay the course. Change and departures from established modes are not easy for Administrators. Winning their commitment usually requires clarifying the reasons for change.   If you have a Style other than an Administrator, you will have to provide more data, structure and rationale then seems necessary for you. But, remember, Administrators are wired differently from you and if you can adjust to their way of operating, you will have a productive and dependable partner. Finally, always lead with data and be as objective and reasonable as possible. Administrators are worried by subjectivity or what they consider as excess.

In dealing with Integrators, always remember to protect and cultivate the relationship. In practical terms, this means dropping into their work area, consulting with them early in the process, pointing out the impact of their efforts on people and always showing respect - for them as well as others. If you fail to keep in touch with an Integrator, especially one who reports to you, he/she will begin to speculate about what's wrong and become distracted and less productive. Further, if your only contact with an Integrator involves trying to get something from them, they will easily conclude that the relationship is weak and that you are using them, rather then partnering with them. Integrators will insist that they like to know how they are viewed – and they do – but they have difficulty with criticism. More often then not, they take corrective feedback personally and have the tendency to amplify the feedback in their mind. When an Integrator falls short, a gentle nudge or suggestion is usually sufficient. They are often very intuitive and can "read between the lines" to understand your concerns and make an adjustment.

Catalysts, the fourth style, are usually a distinct minority in corporate or government environments. People with Catalyst tendencies naturally gravitate to academic or research institutions. As different from each other as the other three styles are, they all pretty much subscribe to the age-old adage "if it ain't broke, don't fix it." On the other hand, a person with strong Catalyst proclivities would say: "if it ain't broke, let's fix it anyway." You see, a Catalyst thinks, even knows, that anything – practice, policy, process or product – could always be better. They think more than the rest of us, and, more significantly, think about issues others overlook. They constantly ask "what if" questions and can alert a group and its managers of possibilities for improvement and renewal. They are never complacent and often traffic in "out of the box thinking." They can inspire and excite others with their ideas and are happy to leave it to others to enact their schemes. They are "big picture" people and find implementation and details boring, even tiresome. It is probably already apparent that a Catalyst can be a valuable member of a team – if managed skillfully. What is required from his/her manager is first of all, an appreciation for the Catalysts' contribution: creative energy. Convey in the way you react to their suggestions and proposals that their commitment and creativity are valued. Show that you can see possibilities in their ideas. Experience has shown Catalysts that only a fraction of their ideas will be implemented – what they need and desire from other managers is not assent, but an appreciative hearing. Find an aspect of their proposal that is attractive and show interest. Conversely, avoid the tendency to say anything like "we tried that once, it didn't work," or "we don't have the resources for that." A Catalyst wants to see that he/she got through, transmitted energy to you." The Catalyst thinks, "Maybe, someday it'll happen." Often, just that possibility is enough.

The Coaching Orientation

Coaching employees is a challenging responsibility demanding flexibility and skill, but helping others to new levels of effectiveness is the essence of being a manager. Jack Welsh, the former GE leader who helped restore that giant enterprise to prominence, once put it well: "I always looked for opportunities to coach." Welsh is suggesting that an effective manager has a "coaching orientation," a mind set, a readiness to say or do something that will guide employees to effectiveness.

The coaching orientation has three elements:

- **Presence**

- **Observation**

- **Involvement**

Presence

To position yourself to be an effective coach you have to become a "presence" to your reports. The words you use, the actions you take and things you pay attention to, all point to certain bedrock convictions at your core. Your reports may regard you as "different" or even unique but you are not a mystery – they know who you are and what you stand for.

To be a presence it is not necessary to reveal deeply private aspects of your personality, but it is necessary that employees are clear about what motivates you and what you want from them. They come gradually to clarity about how you stand on issues vital to life in an organization:

- Your work ethic

- The extent of real cooperation you provide your peers

- Your persistence in the face of obstacles

- Your willingness to give credit to others for results

- The depth of your integrity

- Your openness to feedback

- Your availability for them

- The quality of your listening

- The strength of your alignment with your boss

- Your willingness to confront issues for the good of the organization

- Your use of company resources

If there is a degree of consistency to your actions in these and related areas, you are positioned to coach because you are a presence. Being a presence does not require perfection, but it does require a degree of consistency that is discernable.

It is important to point out that not all of your employees will like everything you do or agree with all your decisions, (presence does not create miracles), but if they know you they will be open to your influence and coaching. For example, if your reports observe you working at achieving a healthy degree of alignment with your boss. If you are open in dealings with him/her, balance respect with candor, give him/her the benefit of the doubt, and refrain from public criticism, your employees will be induced to behave in a similar fashion in their dealings with you. And when you ask for candor and cooperation your requests will ring true because they can see you doing what you are asking of them. You are, to employ the cliché, "walking the talk," you are a presence.

Observation

Isn't it often the case, as a tough, demanding day concludes that a thought arises in all of us: "I wonder if my boss really appreciates all the things I do around here?" Well, that same question comes to your employees as well. If you want to be a high-impact coach, you have to take the time to observe your people doing the work. You have to observe, not to criticize or evaluate, but just to see, to appreciate, to understand. The CEO of the hugely successful men's clothing chain, still finds time to visit stores, sell clothes alongside his employees and during lulls, listens to the salespeople and shares his plans for the company. This practice ensures that he remains a presence to his people and at the same time shows them that he understands their situation – the demands their customers make, and the trade-off's they have to manage. In short, he is present to the challenges of their everyday life. If you, on occasion are there to see, to hear, to observe, your coaching has teeth. Your remarks and suggestions are grounded in their experience.

Observation also helps you bridge the "disconnect" that naturally develops between a manager and the "troops." Losing touch with everyday operations can induce you to make decisions that "don't fit." One senior executive of a major hotel chain who prided himself on "being from the field" but, restricted his site visits to formal, ceremonial tours, fell into this trap. Influenced by data indicating the marketing advantages of the addition of in-room coffee makers in all the chain's rooms, he mandated their introduction (without much field input). When implementation was sluggish and incomplete, he fumed that the field "just doesn't get it," and threatened several hotel managers with disciplinary action. At about this time, I happened to visit a well-managed resort in the system. When I asked the manager about the coffee-maker problem, he marched me to one of his suites, opened the door and barked: "You take a look! Where am I supposed to put a coffee-maker here? There is no space!" Later, over lunch, in a calmer tone he made a request: "I just wish you could get those guys from corporate to come out more often so they could see what we face and understand the impact of their decisions." His request was more than reasonable. He realized that without first-hand contact with the people doing the work, managers lose touch. Their views, decisions and coaching miss the mark. To enable yourself to coach, you have to be there, you have to observe.

Involvement

Managers, with good reason, focus on results. They ask about what was done and when it was done. But a manager who aspires to measurably impact productivity also needs to inquire about the process that was followed – the how. Inviting employees to relate the methods used, the obstacles encountered and skills they displayed opens doors for the manager – coach. By showing interest in the details of an employee's activity, you first of all, demonstrate an appreciation of their undertakings. You show them that you are an interested partner in their organizational endeavors, not just order-giver who adds up profits and losses at the end of the day. But just as importantly, the insights you gain by engaging your people in this way positions you to coach in the future in a relevant and informed way. Your knowledge of their day-to-day activities helps you maintain credibility as a coach, enabling you to offer suggestions that will empower them. Keeping informed allows you to more clearly understand employee's strengths and areas for improvement. Also, you are able to draw parallels between past situations and current ones; to help them see how past breakthroughs can lead the way to future results.

In short, cultivate the habit of asking about the process, the details not just the results. If you do you will measurably increase your impact as a coach.

The Challenge of Delegation

When I ask participants in my "Transitioning from Individual Contributor to Manager" seminars for their biggest challenges, they always include delegation. And they are right. Delegation is challenging, especially for managers who are skilled doers. Because you are probably highly skilled (that's why you were promoted), you hesitate to entrust someone else with a task you could do and do well. On top of that, as we pointed out in the chapter on "Doing Your Old Job," you enjoy doing things. You derive satisfaction from achievement. Delegation entails giving up the fun and satisfaction of doing it yourself. Finally, when you delegate, you retain responsibility for the result while giving up control to someone else. That can be unnerving.

For all the above reasons, you, like most new managers, probably have difficulty delegating. And when you do turn over a responsibility to someone else, you usually use the approach that is natural to, and compatible with, your style. If you are a Director, you tend to give few details and leave it up to the subordinate to chart his/her course. If an Administrator, you probably require that the other provide you with a detailed plan – or you provide one yourself. One way or the other, you insist on clarifying the process. As an Integrator, you probably will be at pains to show the subordinate the importance and meaning of the assignment and will be overly concerned with their reactions – you'll want to make sure they are happy about the task. Finally, Catalyst managers tend to stress the big picture and focus the conversation on the possible impact of the assignment – to the neglect of helpful direction on how to get it done. In other words, we usually either want our people to do it our way or we talk to them the way we prefer to be talked to when we receive an assignment.

To counter these tendencies, it is necessary to focus on the needs of the task and then consider the readiness of the person to do it successfully. Two considerations trump all others: the requirement of the task and the readiness of the person to do it, rather than the dictates of your style (or even the preferences of the style of the other). To delegate successfully follow these steps:

1. Clarify in your own mind, what your intention is. Your intention could be any of the following: job done according to specific requirements, job done quickly, job done error-free. Then again you might make an assignment to test skills of a subordinate or to encourage the development of new capabilities. This step, often neglected by new managers, is critical. The person receiving the assignment deserves to know your expectations, your "conditions of satisfaction," at the outset – not after the fact. Too often new managers have unconscious standards or measures (based on their own experience in doing similar tasks) but do not articulate those expectations. Instead, after the project is underway, or even worse, after the task is completed, they judge the effort inadequate – to the surprise of the employee. Realizing and sharing expectations is not a naturally acquired ability for a former doer who is now a manager. That's because doers just do – they follow their instincts and utilize their experience almost unconsciously. Willie Mays, the baseball star once gave voice to this truth. When asked what accounted for his excellence on the field he simply, and truthfully said: "They throw the ball, I hit it. They hit the ball, I catch it." Explaining something to someone else before the fact is as we say, "a whole different ball game." The Chapter Five, "Watching for Mistakes" will offer some tips on how to's.

2. Reflect on what is needed in terms of skills and resources.

3. Estimate the subordinate's readiness in two dimensions: **Can** and **Will**. **Can** refers to ability, skill or training to perform this task; not overall skill, but skill to do this assignment. **Will** refers to motivation, confidence, willingness to undertake and complete the task.

4. Choose the "high percentage" delegation strategy based on the above analysis.

The four strategies are:

LOW CAN, LOW WILL

DIRECT – Explain what you want done and how to do it. This approach is called for if the person is new to the company or inexperienced in this arena. Their "can" is low, and probably, so is their confidence or "will." The inexperienced person can appear to be confident; perhaps because they were successful in other environments, they are confident. But the confidence is unfounded, so the "will" is, in actuality, low.

UNCLEAR CAN, HIGH WILL

QUESTION - Describe the task and then inquire how he/she would approach it. Your questions are designed to uncover the person's skill and experience level. Motivation here is high, but you need to find out the level of "can." If the approach they come up with indicates low "can", then provide more input; if their plan appears sound allow them a freer hand.

HIGH CAN, LOW WILL

MOTIVATE- Don't waste time and energy showing a person with high "can" how to do it, even if they are not producing. Instead, motivate, elevate the level of "will" by stressing the importance of the assignment to customers, your group, or their standing. Another important element of this strategy is questioning to find the root of the problem. Find out the motivational blocks.

HIGH CAN, HIGH WILL

DELEGATE- Explain what you want, set a completion date and let them succeed. Don't slow down a highly skilled, highly motivated person with unneeded direction or motivation.

An assessment of the "readiness" of a person is, of course, only needed when major assignments are involved. Routine tasks simply don't require much analysis. But if the task is critical, you should take the time to select the most appropriate delegation strategy. The graphic below is a simple and practical guide for busy managers like you.

Readiness Model

The choice of the high percentage delegation strategy will not insure success, but this step-by-step process is vastly superior to what is usually done – delegating in accordance with dictates of our style. The task is where the action is; the demands of the task are paramount.

We all learned that the Golden Rule was the surest basis for conduct: "Do unto others as you would have them do unto you." It is a wonderful guide. Except in some respects it is counter-productive in management. If you speak to others, especially your reports in the manner you prefer, you will miss the mark more often that you hit it. If you delegate tasks, make requests, and deal with problems and conflict the way your style dictates, you will be only marginally effective as a manager. To succeed in management you have to develop flexibility in method, speech and action. You have to connect with your people by altering your approach to get on their wave length. Whether you are a skilled problem-solver (Director), organized analyst (Administrator), diplomatic communicator (Integrator) or creative inspirer (Catalyst) you cannot expect that everyone you manage will be like you or have the same skills. What you can expect is that each member of your team meets or exceeds their job's requirements, in their way. Their way may, and probably will, be different from yours, but their way is not necessarily less effective then yours. Uncover what each employee is good at, help them stretch and develop new skills, coach them to new levels of effectiveness, but avoid the trap of: "my way is the right way." Insisting on your way and delegating only in your way, will distance you from many of your team and lower their productivity. Uncovering everyone's preferences, natural gifts and style, on the other hand, will enable you to maximize their potential and create a real team.

Notes

Chapter Three

Closely observe the work patterns, decision-making and speech of your reports. Determine their Operating Styles.

Adjust your behavior and especially your coaching approach to fit the Style of the employee.

Position yourself to be an effective coach by becoming a "presence" to your employees. Show them, with words and actions, what is your preferred "way to be" in an organization.

Take time to observe employees doing the work to show interest and gain insight into their strengths, challenges and areas for development.

Inquire about the processes and methods they used, not just the result. Such involvement will provide you with valuable data for your coaching and make your comments to them relevant.

Don't delegate the same way to everyone.

Determine the readiness of the employee to do a particular task by assessing his/her "Can" and "Will." Then select a delegation strategy that fits the situation.

Application Assignment

- ✓ Focus on a significant upcoming task or project and select a member of your group to do it.

- ✓ Clarify your intention – why this person, what are your expectations?

- ✓ Assess his/her "Can" and "Will" levels.

- ✓ Choose an appropriate delegation approach.

- ✓ Rehearse what you will say before you make your request.

CHAPTER 4

FAILING TO STAND FOR SOMETHING

Several years ago I joined a twosome of rugged-looking men on a Florida golf course. My golf game on that day was forgettable, but something one of the men said during the round was not. As we approached a tee box on the second nine he pointed to one of the homes that lined the course and informed me that Don Shula lived there, and further, that he once served as an assistant to the great coach. Shula's main claim to fame of course was achieving the only perfect, no loss season in the history of the National Football League. He is regarded not only as a great coach, but as a highly effective leader. My interest was peaked. I asked a number of questions: "What made Shula so effective?" "What was the key to his success?" "What did he do?" The questions, of course, ruined my companion's concentration, but after struggling to articulate his assessment, he paused before a shot and said: "I got it. I know. Nobody worked harder for the team than Shula did." As he elaborated on his observation, he made it clear that Shula consistently "showed up" as committed to his players and to his team – and his commitment was contagious, even inspiring. His coaches and his players watched him and learned from him. They respected his dedication and each in his way came to imitate him. His words stayed with me and eventually I came to realize that a manager like a coach, like any leader, has to stand for something, has to embody values that reflect something of his/her core. And if the values are firm, relevant and backed by a discernible pattern of behavior, they can encourage similar behavior in others. Whether you believe or do not believe that managers should be "role models" it is beyond dispute that subordinates observe, closely observe, their managers – and that they extract lessons from their observations. If you aspire to be not just someone who fills the role, but someone who excels at management, who leads others to excellence, you will have to give serious thought to what you stand for, what you value.

The Power of Example

In my "High Impact Coaching" workshop I ask the participants to name someone from their professional life who changed them by their coaching. They are next asked how the person got the message across. The story is always the same. Every participant reports that it was the person's behavior, their example, that was key. What you say as a manager is, of course, important, but what you do is decisive. How you operate with peers, bosses and reports establishes the norms, creates the guidelines and sets the tone within your group. You have to embody the habits and demonstrate qualities you want from them.

Most of us give scant attention to such matters when we become managers. We just grab the reins and start. But reflecting on rules of conduct that will guide your behavior goes a long way toward determining what kind of manger you will be – and what kind of lessons you will impart to your people.

A discussion of values may seem remote from the everyday world of work in a modern organization – but nothing could be further from the truth. Let me illustrate from my experience as a manager. I began my corporate career in a company that was doing well. We were highly profitable, analysts regularly praised our stock and we sent generous dividends to our investors. "Great," you're thinking, "ideal." And that's close to what we were thinking as well; but we thought we were great. An attitude approaching arrogance spread and gradually morphed into a kind of complacency, even entitlement. Managers who controlled budgets spent freely and their subordinates followed suite. A notable exception was a zealous senior manager, Laura, who preached prudence and practiced rigorous financial restraint. But in a company culture of excess, she was marginalized and regarded by most as "old-fashioned and tight-fisted." But Laura' values and ways of operating got to me. Later, when I was promoted to the ranks of management, I attended a two-day seminar for new appointees. In the course of the seminar senior managers visited to share their insights with us. Laura met with us for only about thirty minutes, but what she had to say struck a cord in me. Essentially, she said that managers are stewards of corporate resources and that we needed to take our financial responsibilities to our shareholders seriously. What she said made sense, especially when she asked us to utilize company resources as though they were our own.

Taking Value Stands

I decided to heed her advice and make a commitment, took a value stand, to be as careful with company resources as I was with my own. When I traveled, I used the restaurants, hotels and modes of travel that I would if I were using my money. In managing the department budget I honestly assessed our needs and avoided the commonly–used practice of "sandbagging" – artificially inflating the needs in order to be able to absorb predictable cuts by bosses. I also avoided the commonly–followed practice of spending money toward the end of the fiscal year in order to "protect" each line item of the budget. More that once, I was advised by "experienced" peers to "spend this year, or they'll reduce your budget next year." I shared my approach to budgeting and spending with my team – and told them why. I didn't preach, but I did explain my rationale, the value that formed the basis of my practices. I hoped that my practices and my attempts at consistent behavior would encourage acceptance and buy-in from them, but I wondered if I was getting through. And then one day, walking to lunch at the company cafeteria with Rich, one of my team, I became convinced of the power of example. While Rich was reporting on a recent company trip he had made to Chicago, he paused and said: "A funny thing happened after the meetings. I walked out of the hotel and looked at all those restaurants in the Loop and the thought occurred to me – 'where would you want me to eat.'" Rich was acknowledging the presence of our commonly held value. I didn't need to be there. Our value, prudent use of company resources, guided him. A value stand by a manager can influence the behavior of others.

The Power of Value Stands

To further clarify the nature and power of value stands let me offer one other real life example. Before I became a manager I noticed the vivid impact my manager had on us whenever he made critical comments about other managers and groups. Criticism of others by our boss seemed to imply to my peers and me that we were given permission to withhold trust and cooperation and even information when dealing with those individuals and groups. It looked to me like the opposite of what a leader should be doing. I promised myself that if I ever became a manager I would not denigrate other managers or groups in front of my people. This was the beginning of a value stand. As a manager I put forward a consistent effort to deal openly and directly with problems and misunderstandings involving other managers and groups.

This understanding proved to be demanding. There were many times when taking a swipe at other parts of the organization would have felt good, but my value stand was a reminder and a guide. I would share frustrations and difficulties with my team, but always led the discussion to a "What am I/what are we going to do about this problem?" I insisted on action and energy rather than being content with passivity and complaints. Whenever members of my team engaged in taking pot shots at others I'd simply ask: "Have you talked to him/her about this?" I was only positioned to coach in this manner by my own consistent behavior. I could not have credibly asked of them what I was not doing myself.

Gradually, (I must admit the process required about a year) the members of my team took to the value. At staff meetings and in one-on-one's that I would overhear, the team members began to remind each other about the best way to deal with inter-group difficulties. A few of them even took to saying things like: "Come on, complaining doesn't move the ball down the field." Slowly, and with varying degrees of consistency, the individuals in the group assimilated the value and what's more important, began to act on it.

What To Do

Deliberate, conscious behavior is the result of a commitment to a value. The surest way for a manager to really make a difference, to lead others, is to settle on a few key value stands. A value stand has to be relevant, meaningful and expressed in observable behavior.

RELEVANT

In order to be relevant a value stand must be related to your duties and related to needs in your environment. The free-spending practices in my first company and the sniping by mangers that was tolerated made my value stands relevant to my job and to the company's culture. Responsible use of resources and conversations with rather than about other groups were practices that were needed at that company at that time and were therefore relevant.

MEANINGFUL

Meaningful refers to an organic connection between you, your core, and the value stand you choose. In other words, your value stands should express something about who you are or want to be. By committing to confront issues with other parts of the organization rather than talk behind the backs of others, I was giving expression to a deeply held belief in teamwork. As an eighth grader I was part of a basketball team that complied a record of 31 wins and only one loss. We excelled because all of us thought and acted like members of a team. We were encouraged to bring out the best in each other and to refrain from negative comments. That experience of cohesion, along with the success we all experienced revealed to me the utility and value of teamwork. My experience of the power of teamwork when I was thirteen was the basis of value stands as an adult manager. I took the stand not just because I believed in it – it was part of who I am. Your value stand, if it is to make a difference and have staying power, has to come from within you. Unfortunately, most corporate efforts at operating a value-driven culture fail because managers are asked to give allegiance to propositions that are both vague and imposed. There is no meaningful link between the published values of the company and what I've been calling the "core" of the individual managers. It's no wonder that most statements of value remain in the company's visitor lobby – safely ensconced behind a pane of glass.

OBSERVABLE BEHAVIOR

A value stand has to be translated into behavior. It is not just a general resolve to, say, "show respect for people." A value stand can be based on such resolve, but has to be about behavior. For example, "respect for people" could be changed into a value stand such as: "I will consistently share important information with my direct reports, withholding nothing that is critical to their and the group's success." Such a value stand has substance, has heft and would result in a pattern of behavior. Rather that "look good" by tailoring information, you would be honest; rather than talk about performance issues with others, you would confront the issues with the person; rather than blame others for difficulties and break-downs, you would acknowledge your mistakes and miscalculations. And by being such a truth-teller you would not only be showing respect for people but showing others how to act and how to be. Value stands can make you a leader.

VALUE STAND EXERCISE

Take a moment to begin the process of formulating a value stand. As we have said, a value stand should be relevant, meaningful and observable. To ensure that the value stand is really something that comes from your core reflect on what you truly love to do when not at work. The activity need not have any connection to management or your work responsibilities. It's something you do because you like it, it "comes natural" to you.

After getting clear about the activity ask yourself or have a friend or partner ask you a series of "Why is that important to you?" questions. This process will eventually lead to the uncovering of a basic value – something as we earlier said "that comes from your core."

Let me illustrate by relating a value stand mentoring session I recently had with a manager at a high-tech company in Texas. I began by asking Fred what was his favorite activity away from work. Immediately he responded with: "I like to hunt on my dad's ranch. I can walk for hours, alone and really feel good!" I then asked, "Why is that important to you?" He said: "I like the quiet." Again, I asked: "Why is that important?" After about five more "Why is that important?" queries, Fred and I saw that he valued initiative, freedom from constraints. This came from his core. Freedom and initiative, define who Fred is. He agreed. He saw that he didn't just believe in initiative, it was part of him. I then asked Fred how he could "stand for initiative," how he could begin to create an environment of initiative in his group. He immediately came up with three or four specific practices that would encourage initiative in his people. He then described how he would begin to foster initiative and how he would measure his success. At the conclusion of the process, Fred looked pleased he had a plan for creating an environment as a manager. An environment that was meaningful to him and would most assuredly be beneficial to his people.

What is your value stand?

Notes

Chapter Four

Focus on a limited number of value stands and regularly measure your behavior against them.

A value stand is a specific promise to yourself to act in a certain way.

Your consistent example can and will move members of your team to adopt the behavior.

A value stand has to be <u>relevant</u>, <u>observable</u> and <u>meaningful</u>.

Application Assignment

   ✓ Formulate one or two value stands to guide your managerial behavior.

CHAPTER 5

WATCHING FOR MISTAKES

The Business sections of most local newspapers, as well as numerous national publications, regularly post and comment on "productivity gains" across the country. The increased output is more often than not attributed to the increased use of technology. There is, of course, no doubt that speedier computers as well as improvements in data collection and analysis continue to contribute to productivity advances. But the real catalysts for increased productivity come from the people making skillful use of the technology. Supervisors and mid-level managers are being asked, no, told, to do more with less —fewer people, and fewer resources in less time. Their efforts are driving productivity.

Today's first line and mid-level manager faces heightened pressures to produce; to get it done quicker and to get it done more economically. The pressure comes by way of senior managers from shareholders, Wall Street analysts and Boards of Directors. This pressure can be a spur to efficiency and even innovation, but it can present the new manager with challenges and pitfalls.

PITFALL ONE: Letting the Pressure Make you Overly Critical

A new manager gets the message quickly – no one has to speak the words out loud – the message is in the atmosphere: "we expect a lot from you, you should expect a lot from your people." High expectations do lead to results, in fact, study after study has shown that high expectations are the prerequisites of excellence. Your own experience probably reinforces this fact: teachers, coaches, parents and bosses who expect more, get more. On the other hand, in the absence of high expectations, mediocrity flourishes. But many times, managers, especially newly appointed managers who are understandably anxious to succeed, take their responsibility for group results too seriously. This attitude in turn produces anxiety and a generally negative slant on things. Managers afflicted with this mind-set focus on what is missing. They see flaws in the efforts of their subordinates and project a pervasive sense of dissatisfaction. By letting the pressure for more and more results get to them, managers become critics who are rarely, if ever, satisfied. Even when they do not openly express their dissatisfaction, their "glass half empty" outlook is apparent. The employees they supervise feel under-appreciated and vaguely discontented. Managers must and should be concerned about their group's results, but the concern has to be balanced by a certain lightness, a grace, a sense of perspective. The words of the poet, T. S. Eliot, should serve as a watchword for the new manager: "Teach us to care and not to care." This is, of course, more easily said than done, but in response to pressure from without, managers have to learn not to create undue and counterproductive pressure within themselves and in their people.

One practical and concrete way to avoid becoming too critical is cultivate the habit of expressing gratitude when people meet or exceed your expectations. Develop the motivating practice of "catching them doing something right." This requires more than invoking that vapid, but often used phrase: "good job." Making "catching them doing something right" effective requires discipline and thought. You have to point specifically to what the person did. For example, if you observe one of your people effectively conducting a project team update meeting and want to point to the specific actions of the employee, you might say: "I noticed how effectively you involved the Production representative on two occasions, by posing direct questions to him." Such feedback has two advantages: it shows you really noticed his/her actions and it encourages repetition. On the other hand, general praise, because it is vague and imprecise, has little lasting impact. A statement such as, "That was a good meeting you ran" gives the employee little guidance about what should be done next time to produce a similar result.

A specific observation by you helps the employee understand the link between his/her behavior and the positive result. And by focusing the employee on concrete actions, you encourage repetition – and continued effectiveness.

Furthermore, such comments create balance – your reports hear from you not just in response to problems. Balance in your observations – noting both what needs improvement and what merits repetition also encourages balance in your outlook. A luncheon conversation I once had in a Des Moines restaurant is relevant here. By luck, I was seated next to a salesperson that had played football at Alabama under the legendary Bear Bryant. He capped off his sports career with the Green Bay Packers and one of the NFL's greatest coaches, Vince Lombardi. When I asked him to compare the two giants, he reached for an analogy. Both coaches, he said, stood next to brick walls and asked you to run through them (high expectations). Bryant, he continued, would accompany his demand with threats: "Fail and you are a loser, a failure in the eyes of home town, the university and entire state." Lombardi, on the other hand, would say: "Run through it, when you get to the other side, you will be a better Green Bay Packer". Lombardi formed himself into a demanding, yet balanced manager of people; so can you.

54

PITFALL TWO: Trying to Stay in the Know about Everything

One of the scariest realities of managing a group comes from the realization that although you retain accountability for the entire group and its functioning, you do not, and cannot, know about everything that is going on. When this realization hits, some new managers react in an understandable, but ultimately defeating way. They ask endless questions, they require frequent reports, they attempt to be personally involved in even routine activities – in short, they turn into micro-managers. Their over-involvement and questioning is a result of their insecurity – they have to approve, they have to be involved, they have to know. All of this restless activity has two predictable results: the managers become fragmented and over-worked and their people feel over-managed. The more inner-directed and entrepreneurial of their employees leave or harbor resentment for being controlled. The more accommodating reports will adjust by avoiding risks and becoming passive. For the supervisors who fall victim to the micro-management syndrome, the nightmare of nightmares is to be asked a question about a project by a boss and not know the answer. They labor under the belief that as manager they have to know everything. The truth is they don't. They do have to know enough to guide and coach when such help is needed, and they do have to stay abreast of "big ticket" projects. But they must learn to avoid intrusive meddling just to assuage their insecurities. New managers should take to heart the seemingly prosaic, yet helpful insight of Sparky Anderson, the only baseball manager to win pennants in both the American and National Leagues. When he was asked for his secrets for success, he was quoted as saying the following: "Well, it took me several years to figure out how to manage a team, but it finally came to me: get good players, and let them play." Many new managers fail to follow Andersen's formula. They inherit or hire good "players" and then don't let them play. Employees require clear direction and coaching when it's needed, but they are slowed by over-management and second-guessing.

PITFALL THREE: Becoming Problem-Obsessed

One of the liveliest and most enlightening exercises of my "Transitioning from Individual Contributor to Manager" workshop involves having newly appointed managers list the payoff's of leading a group compared with being a group member. On some occasions the "Manager" list is quite brief. When this occurs, the groups always react nervously as they face the fact that management is a demanding enterprise with a lot of challenges and few rewards. When I probe a bit, participants inevitably touch on the fact that as managers they get less positive feedback but hear more frequently about problems and breakdowns. Your experience is probably similar. When things go well, you hear little from your boss, peers and reports. However, when deadlines are missed, costs go up, or quality dips, you are the one people come to. Your life as a manager can become problem-centered. For this there is no cure. It's part of the game and can't be avoided. But what can and must be avoided is becoming problem- obsessed, becoming so focused on breakdowns, that you begin to think more about what could go wrong than what you and your group are accomplishing. When this happens, organizational life takes on the colors and contours of a minefield. You become heavy, irritable and less upbeat. You can then develop the habit of talking about problems all the time and you can sap energy from the members of your team.

One antidote to problem obsession is periodic measurement and celebration (privately) of the positive results of your management, as opposed to your technical contributions. This takes some practice since management impact is generally less concrete, and longer term. But if you train yourself to note developments such as the growth of the people you are coaching, the efficiency of your staff meetings, the clarity of the group's objectives, the tone within the group, or your success at delegating, you can gain and retain a healthy and balanced perspective.

Management Functions

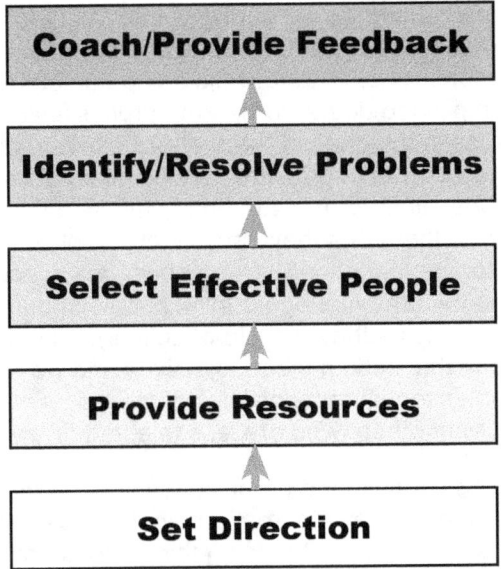

```
┌─────────────────────────────────┐
│     Coach/Provide Feedback      │
└─────────────────────────────────┘
                ▲
┌─────────────────────────────────┐
│    Identify/Resolve Problems    │
└─────────────────────────────────┘
                ▲
┌─────────────────────────────────┐
│     Select Effective People     │
└─────────────────────────────────┘
                ▲
┌─────────────────────────────────┐
│        Provide Resources        │
└─────────────────────────────────┘
                ▲
┌─────────────────────────────────┐
│          Set Direction          │
└─────────────────────────────────┘
```

The above graphic of the critical functions of management can serve as the basis for your self-evaluation. Make use of the model at least quarterly. List the positive accomplishments you and your group have made. Such an exercise will call your attention to the significant long-term impact you are making. Without such periodic reckonings, the day-to-day grind of problems and disappointments that are a part of every manager's life will wear you down and sap your motivation. Making yourself conscious of the subtle, yet significant advances in your management skills and the results they promote will alert you to the positive impact you are having.

At this point you are probably tempted to raise an objection: "Sure, I can see the benefits of reinforcing productive actions and focusing on more than just problems, but there are problems. Sometimes performance is not top flight and issues have to be dealt with!" to which I say, "Right On". The trick is to learn to deal with issues in ways that lead people to new levels of performance. Remember these four steps.

STEP 1: Be Clear About Your Expectations

No new manager ever got in trouble by being too clear about what he/she expected. But being clear at the outset about a job, or even a specific assignment is challenging. The challenge has a two-fold root.

Explaining is different from doing.

New managers are usually, as we earlier pointed out, accomplished doers. Repeated success develops habits and skills that become, for the most part, unconscious. After a while doing something well becomes instinctive. Accomplished doers "forget" the processes of discovery they followed, or, as in the case of "naturals," it came to them almost effortlessly. In the world of sports, the very best players seldom become good coaches. Coaching, for the supremely talented is illusive. Playing well was so easy for them that they can't clearly explain how to do it to the less talented or inexperienced. Deep down, many accomplished professionals who become managers think people should be able to "get it" as quickly and easily as they did. To effectively lead others, managers have to understand that setting clear objectives and well-defined expectations is an essential responsibility of the job. And they must also develop patience with others who are less talented or confident.

Experience in doing things in the organization imparts many skills: how to plan, how and when to deviate from a plan, how to get buy-in, how to obtain needed resources, etc. But doing things does not facilitate the development of a critical managerial skill: clarifying the expected result before beginning. Such clarification has little to do with know-how and street smarts. Nailing down in words the "conditions of satisfaction" for any undertaking is a skill that few individual contributors bring to the job of management . They can spot what's right or what's wrong about an effort that is underway because they have learned mid-course correction maneuvers over the years, but stating what an undertaking should look like, and what the measures should be, has to be learned on the job. Recognizing that you probably didn't know how to set expectations clearly is the first step. Then take specific steps to acquire the skill.

Before making an assignment, write down what the finished "product" would look like. Include time lines, quality markers and all desired specs. Writing down what you want forces you to choose words or phrases that transform a general intention in your mind into something more concrete, defined and specific. Be careful to concentrate on what you want. How is another matter, showing someone how may or may not be helpful or appropriate (see Chapter Two's discussion of delegation). Many times new managers think they are setting expectations when in fact they are describing tactics. Tactics, the how to do it, is usually the strong suit of accomplished doers. Tactics, the how, will often not clarify what you are aiming for – and that's what every employee, no matter how skilled, needs from a manager.

STEP 2: Think Responsibility

Learning how to deal with breakdowns is critical for new managers. At times you will delegate effectively, provide the appropriate resources and assistance, be clear about your expectations – and still not get the desired result. When this happens – and it will happen – you face a moment of truth. Either you will find fault somewhere else: lack of support, inadequate resources, weak motivation in your people or even the "company culture", in other words, "out there," or you will look inside. By looking inside, I mean accepting responsibility for the role you played in the breakdown. Accepting responsibility is not about regret or guilt. Such responses immobilize you and lead nowhere. Accepting responsibility is a matter of confronting a simple question: "What could I have done better?" Managers, who cultivate such a habit of mind, will grow, will learn and will encourage a "can do" attitude within their environment because they are always looking for answers within their sphere of control. Blaming others gets you nowhere. Asking what you could have done differently often yields new possibilities.

Years ago the late George Allen distinguished himself when he took over a floundering professional football team, the Washington Redskins, and quickly built them into champions. The transition was not always easy. In fact in the opening game of his second season as coach, a colossal break – down occurred. His team kicked off to start the game and an opposing player ran through the Redskin defense for a humiliating ninety-five yard touchdown. What made the breakdown all the more galling was the fact that two of his better players badly missed when attempting to tackle the runner. Allen had planned well, traded for good players, consumed hours and hours in instructing his team – and then this. He faced a choice: blame the players or look within. To his credit he looked within. He later reported that during the off-season he asked himself: "What did I fail to do to ready the players?" Out of that inquiry, that "look within," came positive energy for change and a new concept that is now widely used throughout the football world: the Special Teams coach. Teams at all levels now have someone who focuses on selecting and preparing a group of players who specialize in kick-off and punt returns. If Allen had just blamed the players, he probably would have never hit on his idea. By accepting responsibility he turned a Break-Down into a Break-Through.

Step 3: Speak Responsibly

Every manager wants team members to be accountable: to display initiative, be responsive to internal and external customers, fulfill their commitments and keep their promises. When deadlines are missed or mistakes made we all want action and solutions not excuses. We don't want employees who complain about others and blame them for their failures and errors. We want to be surrounded by people who not only act, but speak responsibly.

The foundation for a climate of accountability and responsibility is the speech of the manager. You have to consistently model responsibility in the way you talk. If you blame others, make excuses and absolve yourself when breakdowns occur, so will your people. If, on the other hand, you cultivate the habit of taking responsibility and expressing it with your speech, so will they. It may take time and require on-going coaching from you, but gradually they will learn to talk like leaders and focus on solutions, not blame.

How do you speak responsibly? In matters large and especially when a problem arises, you describe the situation as an "agent' rather than as a "victim". Let's start with some typical "victim" statements and transform them into "agent" statements. Let's say you arrive late for a meeting, the whole team has been kept waiting, you are self-conscious about your tardiness, so you blurt out something like: "I'm sorry, for being late, the traffic on the Interstate was terrible." Now this kind of thing is often said, by us and others. We've come to see it as acceptable, even normal. But what does it really say? It says "I'm not really responsible for being late, the traffic is responsible," i.e. "I'm not an agent, I'm a victim of circumstances beyond my control." Or let's consider another situation even more typical of life in an organization. You consult with your team about a course of action that will make a positive difference for your operation. After examining all the pro's and con's your group reaches a firm consensus. Then you take the proposal to your boss who rejects it as too costly. At the next staff meeting you might be moved to announce something like this: "Well, I ran our plan past Stan and he shot it down." You might even follow this statement with an aside about how tight-fisted Stan is. Now, such a statement is valid and maybe even justified as a way to placate the team and sooth their ruffled feathers, but it contains an undertow of victimhood that can encourage similar statements from the team when they encounter challenges and set- backs. In subtle ways such responses to reversals or challenges by a manager contributes to a culture of blame and resignation.

How do you create a more dynamic results-oriented climate? By a shift in the way you describe your challenges. Instead of the excuse: "the traffic was terrible," you could simple say, "I didn't anticipate the traffic correctly, sorry I'm late." This version reflects a speaker who is an agent. Someone who accepts and expresses his/her role in the situation. The statement conveys accountability and encourages the use of "responsibility speech" in team members.

When reporting the results of your meeting with your boss you could say: "I wasn't able to convince Stan" or "I didn't get across all the advantages of our plan, next time I'll make sure to send him and e-mail first to list all the pluses." These versions suggest accountability and possibility and inject energy into the group, not resignation and passivity.

Start monitoring how often you use excuses or imply blame instead of indicating accountability in the face of problems and reversals. Then start cultivating the habit in your people. For example, if a group member attributes a missed deadline to the lack of urgency displayed by employees in another part of the organization, you could say: "Well, what could you have done to get them committed." or better yet: "What will you do next time to get them to focus on your requests?" Such coaching, however, will only have traction if your team hears you taking responsibility when you report on your difficulties. In short, your modeling, complemented by your coaching will gradually establish a culture of achievement and responsibility.

Step 4: Develop and maintain a Future-Orientation

Managers who produce superior results with and through motivated people possess a "future-orientation." A future orientation has many facets, but primarily involves focusing on possibilities rather that limits; potential rather that problems; the future rather than the past. It has to do with the way a manager views people and situations.

Suppose, for example, someone on your team is a technical whiz, let's call him Chuck. He produces high quality works efficiently and effectively. However, when Chuck has to work closely with others, it's a different story. Members of project teams report that he uses sarcasm and even ridicule in response to contributions they make. Further, it appears that he tends to dominate technical discussions or if the leader fails to rubber stamp his ideas, Chuck withdraws and clams up.

Because you are Chuck's manager, people come to you to register their dissatisfaction. Exposed as you are to a steady diet of negative news you can begin to see Chuck as someone who is not and never will be a team player. Their flaws are part of their character and beyond remediation. But in my experience, such cases are rare. More often, the Chuck's of the world are in need, desperate need of good coaching, and are not getting it. What they do get is a label e.g. "not a team player" and then exhortations (sometimes) by others to "be more cooperative" etc.

Instead, you, as Chuck's manager, could begin to formulate a plan for his development. The first step would be to view Chuck as someone who could be more cooperative who could operate with a team. This, needless to say, is not easy or "natural." What is natural is to stay in step with the pack – all the people around you and Chuck who are resigned, who have given up on him. You, on the other hand, are responsible for his productivity. It is your job to help bring out of Chuck the behaviors of which he is capable, but not utilizing. This is critical: you have to view Chuck as a potential team player and guide him to act as one. You won't get there by just pointing out his deficiencies (although that may be necessary at some point.) What will get Chuck closer to cooperative behavior is positive energy from you – a belief that he can alter his behavior – complemented by requests for specific, positive behaviors.

What might such a request sound like? Well, you might say: "Chuck, everyone knows you're a technical whiz and problem solver; I have a request: at the next project team update meeting, I want you to encourage Chris and Ajit to come up with solutions to the "bugs" in the Alpine package. You know, ask for their input and show support for whatever they come up with that has merit. Your skills for seeing holes in solutions, if implemented with support for others can help them develop their skills. You make contributions now, I want you to multiply your impact by helping others develop. Can I count on you to involve and support Chris and Ajit?"

Will such an approach always work? Well, nothing always works with people. But does it offer new possibilities for improvement compared to what passes for "coaching" such as: "You've got to do better at team meetings," or "stop being so critical!"? You bet! Positive, well-timed requests produce improvement because they are specific and they are positive. They point the way to new patterns of conduct and inject new future-focused energy into the situation.

Notes

Chapter Five

Maintain a positive tone with employees by "catching 'em doing something right."

Be specific: instead of the catch-all "good job," point to a specific action that contributed to the result.

Avoid becoming "problem obsessed" by reflecting on your managerial accomplishments.

Concentrate on mastering the skill of clarifying your expectations before the start of an assignment.

Practice speaking like an "agent" rather than a "victim" to encourage responsibility in your group.

Maintain a future focus: When coaching an employee focus on his/her potential, not just on the problem at hand.

Application Assignment

   ✓   Keep a record for two weeks:

      ✓   Number of times you spoke like an agent vs. like a victim

      ✓   Number of times you "caught 'em doing something right" and pointed to specific behaviors, rather than invoking the "good job" phrase.

CHAPTER 6

FAILING TO CREATE MEANING

Several years ago my car radio picked up a country tune that I heard just once, but it contained a line that has stayed with me since: "You got to stand for something or you'll fall for anything". The line held such resonance for me because it underscored a conversation I had just had with a long-time friend who worked at a large chipmaker in Silicon Valley. His company partnered with a Japanese high tech conglomerate and he had just returned from Osaka. He related some of the insights he obtained during the visit, but it was when he described a short conversation he had in the Japanese company's main lobby that he became animated. It seems that for several days he had noticed an employee there who shined shoes and did so with great gusto and spirit. My friend became so fascinated with the employee and his obviously high level of motivation that he asked his interpreter if he could talk to him. A few minutes into his shoeshine, he hazarded a question. "I mean no disrespect," he said, "but I've noticed you working here everyday and also noticed how enthusiastically you go about your tasks – in my country an employee who shined shoes would not be as highly committed as you apparently are". After the interpreter finished speaking, the man paused and replied: "Oh, you see, I don't shine shoes, you see, our salesmen and executives visit customers to present our fine products and if their shoes are not clean, the customer may not respect our company and our products. You see, I don't just shine shoes". After he finished the story my friend paused and then added his own take on the experience: "That guy", he said, "has a manager"! And indeed he has, a manager who knows the real meaning of work and communicates that meaning to his employees. He knows the difference between laying bricks and building a home.

His story and the line from the country song both pointed to the importance of meaning at work. Managers, if they are to lead and not just direct traffic, have to reach deep and uncover values and articulate meaning. It is the job of every manager to explain the WHY, the significance of work.

Of course this runs counter to prevailing practice in most companies. Most think it is up to the CEO or the President of the firm to talk about such matters. In truth, few company heads do so, or when they do venture into the realm of meaning, when they attempt to describe the goals and aspirations of the enterprise, they reach for shop-worn and empty phrases that are general, unconvincing and empty. Speaking to technicians who want to make the world work, scientists who studied in order to uncover truth, engineers who desire to create solutions or salespeople who desire to provide new resources to their customers – speaking to such employees, most corporate leaders "inspire" them with calls to be "best in class", "first to market" and ask them to dedicate themselves for the sake of "shareholder equity". To be fair, that's about the best the top people can do. When talking about the "why" of the company, the average CEO has to be mindful of multiple constituencies; security analysts, investors, competitors, the government, and the employees. Forced to cast such a wide net, senior leaders are driven to the general and ultimately to the inconsequential. That leaves it up to the group leaders, to managers at the grass roots level to create meaning.

Managers have to realize that although employees come to work in order to make house payments, provide food and necessities for their families and educate their children, they also come to work to make a difference. People want, in fact, need to feel that their efforts are significant and that their contributions mean something. And it is their immediate manager who has to provide that meaning. Managers must explain the company's role in the world, the significance of its products and services and the part played by the group in making it all happen.

Explaining the Role of the Company

It has become fashionable to imply and even to openly state that companies exist to make a profit. Participants in my management seminars frequently give voice to this position and seem to do so proudly. They often appear to be attempting to be hard-headedly practical in asserting that it's "all about money!" But if the grim scandals, bankruptcies and outright thievery in even major corporations during the waning years of the previous century have demonstrated anything, they showed what can result when profits are held up as the main goal, as the reason for being, of an institution. Focus on profits to the exclusion of other aims encourages skullduggery and shrivels the humanity of those who call the company their home.

Profits, rightly viewed, are a by-product. By that I mean not that profits are insignificant, but that profits come about as a result of something else: fulfilling or exceeding the needs of customers. Products and services become successful when they fill apparent or even unconscious needs in the world. When a company creates such products and services, produces them well, sells them effectively, and tends to its customers, those customers will reward the provider with revenue – and with profits. Helping customers is the real reason for companies. When managers talk about the enterprise they should make it clear how his/her each employee contributes to the group mission of meeting and exceeding customer needs. Group and individual objectives should be tied to the grand undertaking of making the world work by helping customers. Work, properly appreciated and described is noble, is significant, and is meaningful. Dedicated, loyal employees are deserving of nothing less than authentic articulations of purpose that go beyond calls for profit. You won't be able to articulate the meaning of the company and the meaning of working there until you take seriously your responsibility for explaining purpose and do the work of clarifying in your own mind, what you think the company means and what the company is finally there to do.

This discussion may sound a bit elevated and abstruse, so let me use an example from my own experience as a manager to show how meaning can be addressed. When I was a mid-level manager, I was sent to a two-day meeting in another state. After spending the entire first day entombed in a hotel conference room with uncomfortable chairs and no windows, I needed to take a walk – a long walk. My route took me to a busy intersection with a quick-changing pedestrian light. As I was about to race across, I noticed an elderly woman with a walker apprehensively eyeing the menacing cars and their aggressive drivers. I helped her cross and when we reached the other side, I complemented her for "being out and about." In reply she explained that walking was now so much easier because her doctor had provided her with a prescription that eased her joint pain – and then she named the drug – one that my company marketed (at the time it was the leading arthritis medicine in the world). On the flight back as I gazed at the towns and cities we passed, I thought of all the people down there that our products were helping – and then I shared my traffic story and airplane reflections at my next staff meeting. I simply reminded everyone in the department that we were part of a company that was making a real contribution to the world and that our jobs meant something. That's what I mean by creating meaning.

Without an articulation of the big picture, the view from 30,000 feet, employees will focus on their own small plot and lose sight of what the company is doing for the world. When perspectives get narrower and more constrained, people become smaller and can descend into pettiness and counter-productive rivalries with other parts of the organization. The creation of meaning can do more than motivate. Reminding people about the impact of your company's products and services can encourage team work and real inter-group collaboration. Start-ups often embody and reflect a clear sense of mission – usually because of the very real presence of the founder. A founder came with energy and authenticity and explained the why of the company. He/she can relate stories about the creation and formation of the enterprise. A founder can clarify the needs he/she saw in the world and outline how the company plans to satisfy those needs. As a result the energy and collaboration in most start-ups is high. People do what is needed for the whole company and its customers. Instead of asking: "Is this in my job description?" They just do it – for the sake of the firm.

In older, more mature organizations, this sense of mission, this clarity about meaning, fades. Only individual managers can revivify it. One of the most practical ways you, as a manager, can create meaning for your group presents itself at goal-setting time.

When you assemble your team to plan for the coming year, never fail to discuss the importance of the group and its contribution to the whole. Keep team members aware of the needs of your most important internal and external customers by encouraging feedback from them and conveying the information to the group. Create a simple mission "statement" – in your own words that captures the essence of the group's role in the company. The mission "statement" can be informally phrased – you have to be comfortable enough with it to be able to repeat it often, and it should be brief and compelling. One sales manager I know likes to remind her people that "We don't sell chips, we help customers find solutions." A very effective HR leader often repeats this mantra: "We're here to ensure that our employees are led by fair and skillful managers."

Frequently challenge the team by asking them to rate their performance against the expectations of customers or groups within the company. Especially at goal-setting time ask for ideas and initiatives that would improve the group's effectiveness in the eyes of the company. Employing such tactics encourages responsible leadership in your people and keeps them attentive to the needs of other groups. Managers who create meaning break down the silos that obstruct teamwork and discourage the defensiveness and myopia that groups can develop. You can also encourage healthy self-appraisal in the group by asking for feedback from them. In my one-on-one's throughout the year and more formally at performance appraisal time, I would ask each team member to identify three to four actions by me that helped and a similar number that hindered them or detracted from their effectiveness. Once they realized that I would listen and that no negative consequences would come to them, they began to provide me with avenues for my improvement as a manager as well as ideas for improving the whole team's efficiency. The meta-message that the process of asking for feedback provided was even more significant then any particulars: I was there to help them be effective, they were there to help the group reach its goals. This is the stuff of meaning.

Finally, as their manager it is up to you, at performance review and through the year to underline the unique contributions each person in the group is making. Again, specificity is key. Instead of saying, "you are an excellent designer", point to a specific event or project and underline the unique contribution make: "You demonstrated real creativity in debugging the Alpine system for the Xercom people. I look forward to more efforts like that. You helped the customer and our whole group." Coaches of sports teams always make sure that everyone understands their role in team success – so should you.

Another way you can create meaning and at the same time provide direction for your group is to formulate a broad strategy. A group's strategy differs from its goals. Goals state what you aim to accomplish; a strategy, on the other hand, describes how you aspire to operate, and how you want to be viewed by your internal customers. Your group strategy contributes to the creation of a team's identity and can be the foundation of real esprit de corps. By real esprit I mean dedication to an ideal, a way of showing up, not silo-thinking or defense of turf. In the absence of a clear strategy, groups often gravitate toward inwardness and group-think. "We're right, they're wrong" or variations of such thinking can take over a team that lacks the direction of a strategy. At this point it is probably necessary to describe possible strategies for your group.

Most well-run companies have a basic strategy that is often indicated by their print and TV ads. When WalMart ends its commercials with "Lower prices, always," their strategy is apparent: we will focus on efficiency and cost cutting. On the other hand when the home improvement company, Lowe's, states "Together, we can build it" they indicate that their focus will be on service and responsiveness. BMW's manta, repeated in every ad, "The Ultimate Driving Machine" announces their strategy: we are dedicated to providing well-engineered vehicles. These three examples could be multiplied, but they suffice to illustrate the three main strategies for a company or a work unit like yours:

- **Efficiency, reliability, cost, effectiveness**

- **Responsiveness, customer focus, service**

- **Innovation, creativity, initiative**

While other strategies are possible, these three are broad enough to fit most operations. Now, let's take a closer look at these three to help you choose the one that is most relevant for your group.

Efficiency

This strategy applied to a work group implies high quality, cost consciousness and reliability. It is most appropriate for groups with clear responsibilities that follow well defined processes. The other strategies, responsiveness and creativity, while not entirely neglected, are not as important as smooth, error-free operation. Making this strategy work requires not merely its articulation, but managerial focus as well. If efficiency is to be your group's strategy it will be necessary for you and the group to identify your most critical processes and to create metrics for them. Measurement and maintenance of focus will be key: by continually identifying current strengths and weaknesses in the functioning of the group you create the framework for successfully implementing efficiency. Setting high expectations will be your most critical managerial function. "Better, faster" should be your constant request. You will also have to pay close attention to how the work is divided and how your group is organized. Role clarification is, of course, critical since ambiguity and overlapping responsibilities cut into efficiency.

Key Management Activities: Efficiency

- Set high expectations

- Clarify key processes

- Establish metrics

- Track and "publish" results

- Reward reliability

- Identify strengths and areas for improvement

- Keep members focused

- Clarify roles, attend to structural issues

- Recruit team members who are detail-oriented and who value quality

Responsiveness

This strategy is most appropriate for groups who provide services, information or expertise to other parts of the organization or external customers. Responsiveness is, or should be the strategy for staff functions, sales departments and IT groups. Such teams will need to maintain an external focus. Periodic surveys and customer focus groups will be critical for two reasons: valuable information about customer satisfaction will keep members focused on the right issues and, more generally will promote an awareness or sensitivity to service issues.

As the manager of a group focused on responsiveness, it will be critical for you to consistently convey feedback from others in an accommodating, non-defensive manner. Years of consulting with corporate groups such as IT or HR have alerted me to the fact that data collection is not enough: listening and responding to customer expectations and reactions is necessary. And this will not always be easy, for you or your team members. But at all costs, you, as the leader will have to resist the temptation to discount customer input. Responsiveness will not flourish in a group whose boss reacts like one IT Director I once worked with. Confronted with specific and highly critical input that internal customers had provided, he looked at his team and said, "Well, which IT group ever satisfies everyone?" or an HR Vice President who told her staff that was struggling to respond to a negative survey: "They obviously don't understand the way we work." While you may not be able to respond exactly the way a given customer wants, it will be important that you consistently convey to customers and team members a willingness to listen and make alterations.

Key Management Activities: Responsiveness

- Establish channels for customer feedback

- Involve key customer – contact team members in the analysis of feedback

- Reward members of team who excel in meeting/surpassing customer needs

- Consistently model receptiveness; avoid defensiveness

- Recruit service-oriented people

- Set annual customer satisfaction targets

- Create and maintain extensive peer networks

Innovation

Every department or work unit needs innovation and creativity. Groups lacking those qualities stagnate and decline. But some groups are looked to primarily as catalysts, sources of change and new ideas, because every company needs people who look beyond the present into the future. Business Development, Marketing, and Research groups have to pose questions, test assumptions and pull the organization in new directions. Employee Development groups that are successful operate in this mode as well. If your group's role is to launch new programs and initiate change then Innovation should be your central strategy.

But managing Innovation is tricky especially because you need to maintain a balance between maintenance, attention to the near term, and creativity, focus on the new and untested.

As manager you will at times appear "inconsistent" to your people because you will have to reign in their horses in order to bring projects to completion and respond to short term needs. And yet all the while you have to be dedicated to establishing and maintaining a climate of questioning and innovation. Striking and preserving that balance is demanding. Let's first consider how to establish an innovative atmosphere.

Creating a Climate of Innovation

The climate starts with you. You have to embody innovation by adopting a mode of operation as a manager that allows questioning of practices, even your practices. I'm not advocating mob rule, you still are responsible for the group and its actions, but you will have to move beyond the model of manager that most embrace and follow. Even managers committed to a participative approach ultimately act like conductors of an orchestra. They select the scores, assign roles, and determine the tempo. While this management model is appropriate for most groups, a leader of a team focused on Innovation has to operate somewhat like the lead musician of a jazz band. He/she frequently, but not always, sounds the opening theme, but sees leading as the blending of the free-flowing energies of each player. The individual talents and unique strengths of each person has to be identified and cultivated. Freedom rather that conformity has to be encouraged, so at times you will have to show flexibility in the application of policies (within limits). Your meetings should allow and encourage shared discussion making and brainstorming. Don't waste time and energy protecting your positional power and privileges. The ancient words of the Lao Tsu, the Chinese sage, should be your guide:

> When the poor leader leaves, the people say, "Good, now we can accomplish things."
>
> When the good leader leaves, the people say, "He/she accomplished much."
>
> But when the master leaves the people say, "We accomplished much, we did it ourselves."

The **innovative** manager has to aspire to think and act like a master.

Providing Direction and Balance

In order for creativity to flourish, the catalyst group you manage needs some direction. This apparent paradox makes complete sense when you reflect on it. Overarching goals, a few bedrock values, articulated by you establishes the context for creativity and independent action to take place. Your goal setting should be limited to a few objectives – but they should be treated as "must do" by you and the team. These key goals will help the members maintain focus and provide the foundation for other initiatives. Creative people like to theorize, sometimes to the neglect of the hard work of completion. As one highly intuitive professional once confessed to me: "Sometimes I think talking about something is the same as doing it!" Such employees can make a difference and produce real results – if their manager assists them in maintaining focus.

Key Management Activities: Innovation

- Adopt a "jazz band" model of management

- Encourage brainstorming

- Allow questioning of group and company practices

- Avoid defending traditional management prerogatives

- Reward creativity

- Ensure on-time completion of key objectives

- Limit number of key goals

- Recruit creative people

Notes

Chapter Six

Reflect on the impact of your company's products and services.

- *What do they enable your customers to do?*

- *What problems do your offerings help overcome?*

- *Look for examples of the company's impact and begin relating these contributions to your group.*

Remember, keeping employees focused on the big picture helps promote team work and inter-group cooperation.

Application Assignment

✓ Practice articulating meaning. By expressing, in your own words, what your company does for its customers.

✓ Seek feedback from at least one or two employees in your next one-on-one.

✓ Create a succinct way of expressing the "mission" of your group. Try it out at goal setting time.

✓ Periodically solicit feedback on your managerial practices:

- Ask for 2 or 3 actions by you that help them.

- Ask for 2 or 3 that distract them or get in their way.

✓ Choose a strategy that is appropriate to the work of your group.

- Efficiency

- Responsiveness

- Innovation

✓ Begin employing the management practices listed to support a group "culture" that compliments the strategy.

CHAPTER 7

NEGLECTING STREET SMARTS

"Street Smarts" refers to the ability to ascertain and adjust to a given organization's culture. It means figuring out how to adapt within an environment in order to be effective. Cultivating Street Smarts involves getting clear about issues such as: how to present ideas, negotiate with peers, communicate with bosses, act at meetings and deal with problems. Every organization has norms which must be honored, and others that can be bent. Street Smarts guide a new manager through this confusing thicket of do's and don'ts. Street Smarts clarifies how you, with your unique gifts, abilities, and tendencies can reach a satisfying "dialog" with the culture and maximize your impact in the organization you have joined.

Acquiring Street Smarts would appear an easy matter - all a new manager has to do is observe. But it's not nearly that easy. Looking around will yield some confusing and at times contradictory messages. You will observe some managers who are courteous, others who are brusque; some who speak up at meetings, others who remain quiet; some that form open partnerships with peers and bosses, others who withhold information and loyalty. The trick is to rummage through this disorderly cultural warehouse of behaviors, beliefs and attitudes to come up with those on which there is tacit agreement. In its most basic formation a culture's norms can be summed up as: "Around here we...." This discovery process is challenging because the truly essential norms are unspoken. To uncover them and adapt, follow these four steps:

STEP 1: ACKNOWLEDGE THE NEED FOR ADJUSTMENTS

"No man is an island" is an often-used line of a seventeenth century poet; it is also a truism every new manager should keep in mind. Whenever you move from individual contributor to manager, from one business unit or division to another or from one company to another – you will have to make alterations. This is not to say that you have to shed your personality, abandon your principles and become a spineless conformist. It does mean that in order to succeed in a new environment you will have to adjust to the imperatives of that environment. I once observed a talented marketing manager who can serve as a good illustration of what I'm getting at.

Jim came to our company from an organization with a fairly aggressive, almost confrontational, culture. People at all levels, but especially managers, were expected to ask tough questions at meetings and to advance their ideas with vigor and energy. Our company was very different. It was a highly profitable concern that dominated a niche in the industry, generated big profits and was comfortable, even complacent with itself. In addition, the company's founder was a cultivated and courteous person who modeled collaboration and decorum in all things. He could probe for information but so smoothly and skillfully that you were never uncomfortable in his presence. I was present at a company celebration in Mexico at which a secretary confidently asked the founder to dance. Would that happen with your CEO? In a company that reflected the chairman's style, Jim's hard charging, in-your-face manner did not serve him well. He occupied an important position in Marketing, and had to interface with people and groups throughout the company, but Jim never figured out how to adjust. He alienated his boss, a couple of VPs and most of his staff. Jim was befuddled. He was following the compass that provided him with direction at his old company. But nine months later he was gone.

Everyone, including you, has to acknowledge the need for adjustments when you change roles or environments.

STEP 2: DETERMINE WHAT IS REWARDED, WHAT IS CRITICIZED

The best method for clarifying the rewards/punishments system of an environment is to listen – carefully – to what opinion setters, especially well-placed managers, say about other people. Most new managers make the mistake of interpreting comments about others as irrelevant to them. Nothing could be further from the truth. When others are being talked about, when their actions and habits are being evaluated, **you** are being addressed. If you pay attention you will receive invaluable data about what is noticed and rewarded or shunned by the environment. New managers (as well as new arrivals) should pay attention to the behavior patterns of "comers" and people in important positions who are generally regarded with respect. Listening to what is said about them will clarify critical norms.

Get clear about how to influence others – "Head push" vs. "Belly push"

In all environments, no matter how collaborative or team oriented, there is "pushing"; people attempting to get agreement, support or action from others. Most organizations evolve a preferred influencing style: reliance is placed on either facts, data and analysis (Head) or experience, intuition and power (Belly). While no company relies solely on "Head" or "Belly" push, close observation will indicate a preference that you should honor. Observe skilled influencers. Take note of how they "push". Adapt their techniques to your Operating Style and then experiment in meetings, conferences with bosses, peers and reports. Initially, your close observation of attempts to influence will probably result in bewilderment because at first you will see only variety. But it will be helpful to you to note how the most admired managers influence and negotiate. Your detective work will of course uncover exceptions- well-placed people who follow their own drum beat and employ methods that diverge from company norms. Herb was a powerful regional V.P. who succeeded almost in spite of himself. While most key managers used "Head Push" but in a cultured and polite way, Herb often resorted to a "Belly Push" style. He was not above using ridicule on subordinates and even seemed, at times, to revel in dominating others. With peers he could be charming but also sarcastic, even caustic. Yet Herb was almost wildly successful. His region always made its numbers and he got fat bonuses. But because Herb was out of sync with the company's influencing norms his standing was completely dependent on his quarterly results. Had he not produced, his style would have defeated him. The important point here is that you should pay attention to the influencing styles of successful managers who are also admired – they and not the Herb's of the world reflect an organization's norms.

Watch how Information is handled: Red Cross vs. Citibank

In any organization, information is a valuable currency. You can use it to get things and share it to generate trust. Note how freely people provide information about their operation; how open they are about potential problems; how forthcoming they are about their plans. Again, you will see plenty of variation here, but close observation of how key managers react to others who are either open or tight – lipped will indicate your organization's preference. Is your environment like the Red Cross – providing assistance to those in need – or like a giant bank where information is doled out very carefully and sparingly?

Work Ethic – "Just do it" vs. "Stay balanced"

Everyone, it seems, works hard these days. Global competition has made it an imperative. Even formerly protected monopolies like the phone company and government agencies like the Department of Motor Vehicles are demanding more of their people. And the quality movement has created new levels of expectations in customers and forced organizations to "get it right, every time." But in some companies hard work has become a badge of honor. Sacrifice and long hours are the primary indicators of commitment and effectiveness. In such environments managers are expected to establish high standards and insist on them at all costs. Other companies will withhold rewards for supervisors who push their people too hard. Such firms want results, but want employees who balance their work and private lives. Watch other managers operate; see which ones are promoted. Listen to the stories related by people who are advancing. Are they studded with: "I told her to…", "I got him to…", if so you probably have a culture of "Just do it." Firms standing for balance will observe something close to traditional hours and protect employees with helpful programs and policies. In such climates overbearing managers will hear from the people-oriented HR group about their conduct. Again, listen, observe and adjust.

Locate the Primal focus:
"Doing it Right or Doing it Right Now"

Some companies or divisions within companies value process, the way something is done. Generally, all "stakeholders," persons and groups that will be affected by the undertaking, decision or change will expect to be consulted or at least informed. Collaboration is stressed and continuity is valued – reference to the past is advantageous - it shows, "respect" for what has gone on before. At times parts of the organization may hold off support or resources because the initiator did not enlist them in traditional ways, or because the new thing, whatever it is, doesn't, to their mind, "fit." Proactive leadership is possible in such climates, but only if exercised with sensitivity to "the way it's done here." I once consulted with a new manager of a world-class metropolitan hotel. Shortly after assuming command, he announced (against my advice) a top-to-bottom shake up of the operation. My acquaintance with the staff and the hotel's sense of tradition led me to caution him against what he, himself, dubbed "the flame thrower" approach to renewal. The official name of his sweeping initiative was called "Excellence Starts Now." In spite of his enormous talent and boundless energy his renewal effort was pretty much a party of one. Six months later he sent me a long e-mail outlining his new, more gradual approach. The new effort was steered by a committee and was called "A Return to Greatness." Visiting the hotel a year later, I could see improvements throughout the place. By valuing the past and the staff's traditions, he enlisted support.

In other cultures such gradualist approaches will be viewed as "excessive politicking" or even weakness. In such places, product life cycle, competitive pressure or the style of the top person will dictate that "quick" is better than "right." One CEO of a prominent tech company is fond of saying: "Whatever you're doing, do it faster" – and he is not kidding.

It is critical for you to determine if yours is a "right" or "right now" environment.

Gauge the attitude toward authority: "Yes, sir" vs. "I don't think so, Opie"

The ways senior executives are dealt with and spoken to tend to permeate the entire organization and set the guidelines for dealing with authority at all levels. Individual bosses may, of course, depart from the prevailing norms and prove to be more/less approachable, open or informal, but a newly appointed manager does best by "playing the averages" and adhering to the accepted rules for dealing with "superiors."

There are still pockets of "militaristic" operations, but broader cultural changes in society and the impact of enlightened business schools has all but eradicated pure "Yes, sir" cultures. Yet many companies embody norms that are related to the military model. In these companies it is bad form to bring up sticky questions, challenge decisions or speak candidly to managers. And it is career-endangerment to argue with someone higher on the pyramid. In one hotel company where I consulted for five intriguing, and sometimes frustrating years, the wishes and preferences of the top guy, who happened to be a relative of the founder, were never questioned. The process I observed at one Operating Committee meeting illustrates the workings of a paternalistic "yes, sir" culture. The meeting opened with a snazzy presentation by Marketing on an extensive study of customer wishes regarding the bathroom amenities the hotel chain provided. The data clearly showed a preference for less clutter on the sink top and many guests voiced annoyance at having to deal with separate shampoo and conditioner bottles in particular. One of the Regional VPs voiced what everybody was thinking: "It's clear we need to switch to a shampoo that contains conditioner; that's what our customers want." His comment was quickly followed by one from the boss that ended the discussion: "I don't like conditioners in my shampoo." And that was that. In such a culture taking on a boss, any boss, will probably not work.

In other environments, debate is welcomed, even expected. In such organizations, "going along" will be viewed critically. People who accept the status quo and merely comply will be viewed as non-contributors with limited career horizons. Observe well-informed managers. If they feel comfortable advancing initiatives or questioning prevailing practices, you have an open, give and take culture and should experiment with coming forward with your ideas. Ron Howard has gained stature as a director over the years following an acting career that began as pre-teen member of the "Mayberry RFD" cast. In one of his first films he faced the daunting task of directing a cast of elderly and experienced actors in

"Cocoon." In one critical scene he stopped the action and demonstrated how he wanted a line delivered. The veteran cast, clearly uncomfortable with his approach quieted for a moment, they broke into belly laughs when one of the most senior members quietly said: "I don't think so, Opie!" This reference to Howard's adolescent TV character was deft. Howard got the message and from that point on leaned heavily on the input of his skilled and experienced cast. If yours is an environment that is as open as the one Howard apparently created, don't hesitate to voice the corporate equivalent of "I don't think so, Opie."

STEP 3: RECOGNIZE THAT YOUR "DOER" SKILLS WON'T BE SUFFICIENT

Shifting to the mentality and mode of operating a manager is, as we have already pointed out, challenging for all individual contributors. The toughest test faces those who are promoted within the unit they served as an individual contributor. They have to cease for the most part, relying on the behaviors that got them the promotion and figure out what alterations they will have to make to succeed as managers.

The environment remains the same, but the expectations shift dramatically. The style forged as doer may not work as a manager. The fate of a former colleague of mine will illustrate this point. Bill, as an individual contributor, was hard working and tireless. He would undertake major challenges and deliver on time – every time. He was a hard charger and his energy made up for any political missteps he made. He consulted with his boss only on rare occasions and because he produced high-quality results, the boss was basically satisfied. But in the process of racking up victories and gaining considerable visibility, Bill was evolving a "lone wolf" style. Some of his co-workers – out of envy or justified peek at Bill's semi-independent ways, came to quietly resent him. Every time I see a re-run of the movie "Patton," I think of Bill. He and the famous general were cut from the same self-confident, inner-directed cloth. And like Patton, Bill wore a Teflon coating. His results swallowed up his gaffes. Then Bill got promoted.

As a manager he did some things well: his hard work and determination inspired the same in his people, but Bill never created a team. His management style encouraged the development of "other Bill's." His one-on-one's were perfunctory, his staff meetings brief and silted and his goal setting and direction were spotty. He relied on his improvisation skills, honed as a doer, in a role that demanded structure, attention to the needs of his people and diplomatic skills. Accustomed to getting by on his own, he failed to cultivate peer relationships. Other managers, that he saw as less dedicated were dismissed and ignored by him.

Corporations are filled with managers who have a style different from Bill's but who remain mediocre supervisors because they continue to rely on their individual contributor mode of operating. Fortunately for Bill, his group, and the company, a drastic downsizing and reorganization provided him with a slot more suited to his inclinations.

Bill's story should not be taken to indicate that certain styles are unsuited to management, but rather that assets as an individual contributor, if not adjusted in the face of the demands of the new role can be counter productive. His error was to continue to focus on the messages the organization was sending about doing rather than listen for guidance about successful management.

STEP 4: DETERMINE THE SKILLS AND PRACTICES YOU WILL NEED TO MASTER

One last bit of useful advice: LOOK OUT THERE: figure out what creates results and gets rewarded and, LOOK WITHIN: assess your skills and habits in the light of the demands of the new environment. (Remember: even if you are promoted within your business unit or even old work group, because you are now a manager, your "environment" is now different.) The same advice is even more relevant if you switch companies. The rules will change and you will need to re-evaluate your "tool kit," to determine the habits, practices and skills that you will need in order to survive and thrive. An acquaintance of mine found out how important such a re-evaluation was when he moved from the "gentlemanly" culture of a profitable health care company to a hungry conductor firm. His new environment was much tougher and more demanding. But Frank, a bit tone deaf to the new "rules" because of his justifiable pride in his previous track record, failed, in spite of his considerable talents, to adjust. He was asked to leave after only six months.

The most practical way to start these adjustments is to study managers who are proficient in the areas you are weak in. At about the mid-point in my professional career I accepted a position in an international firm led by a very cosmopolitan senior management team. To a person they were seasoned and demanding. If you were invited to a meeting or asked for an opinion, you were expected to come through – forcefully.

My "tool kit" was well stocked with diplomatic, rapport-building skills that had served me well and led to a series of promotions – in my previous environments. Now, I needed more directness and vigor. I looked around – and found a good model in Paul. Under a veneer of politeness and charm, Paul possessed an old-fashioned, East Coast crustiness and no-nonsense style. Our differences, Operating Styles and backgrounds, made copying his approach nearly impossible, but it was unquestionably true that he was successful in this environment and that I needed to change. I began closely observing him in a number of situations. I noted not just things he said, but how he said them, how he looked when he spoke and how others reacted to him. The key to his effectiveness I spotted quickly. Whenever Paul would confront an issue, critique a statement or point out the weaknesses of a proposal, he spoke with a level and measured tone. He betrayed no impatience or irritation or emotion even when delivering what on its face was a potentially withering comment. It was as though he were reporting certitude and had no need to add heat or suggest subjectivity. "This," he seemed to be saying, "is just how it is." And most people listened and often acted on his direction. Paul's style differed greatly from mine, but he opened up new possibilities for me. After observing him win arguments, redirect meetings and confront individuals successfully, I tried my hand at my version of Paul's approach. I experimented first in low risk situations away from work and then gradually interjected assertiveness into my speech with reports, peers and even bosses. Eventually, the skill became easier to access – and helped increase my effectiveness as a Manager.

Your environment and your skill set have to mesh. Insisting on your way of operating, because it worked before, is a recipe for ineffectiveness. Again, it should be stressed that soul-numbing conformity is not being called for here – you should remain true to your basic values and principles. But to connect with the people in an environment, you will have to be alert to stylistic norms and make the appropriate shifts.

Notes

Chapter Seven

Managers who are both successful __and__ admired can reveal a culture's tacit norms.

Get clear about norms regarding:

- *Dealing with authority*
- *Influencing peers*
- *Managing people*
- *Ideal work ethic*
- *Sharing information*

Most cultures evolve a "Head Push" or "Belly Push" style. It is critical to reach clarity on this issue.

Remember that your past success as a "doer" or member of another company may not be an adequate guide in your new situation. Be willing to adjust.

Application Assignment

✓ Determine which aspects of your style need adjustment in order for you to be effective in your environment.

✓ Identify two or three behaviors or habits you will need to develop to adapt to your organization.

✓ Select a few managers who skillfully utilize the behaviors you lack. Closely observe them and gradually adopt those habits by experimenting.

Afterword

The principles and practices covered in this guide should equip you to deal with the challenges of becoming an effective manager, but as your own experience has taught you, management is not easy. It demands self-awareness, a willingness to learn, and the consistent use of specific skills.

Our emphasis here has been on presenting material that could be immediately put to use on the job. If you simply read through the chapters and chose not to work through the "Application Exercises," I strongly urge you to do so over the next few weeks. Reading alone does not enhance management skills. Reflection, followed by experimentation and on-the-job application will ensure improvement.

While we have often noted the challenges of being an effective manager and stressed the difficulties encountered in adjusting to the position, it is also worth pointing out that the role of manager "forces" one to grow. Because you now have broader responsibilities and are accountable for the productivity of others, you have to learn how to further develop your strengths and gradually overcome your weaknesses. In addition, you will have to master new approaches and develop flexibility. All of that adds up to growth.

If you apply the practices we've explored and remain open to feedback, you will succeed. Your boss, your reports and peers, and your customers are depending on you.